EUROPEAN PROBLEM STUDIES

HOLT, RINEHART AND WINSTON

THE UNIFICATION OF ITALY, 1859-1861

Cavour, Mazzini, or Garibaldi

Edited by CHARLES F. DELZELL

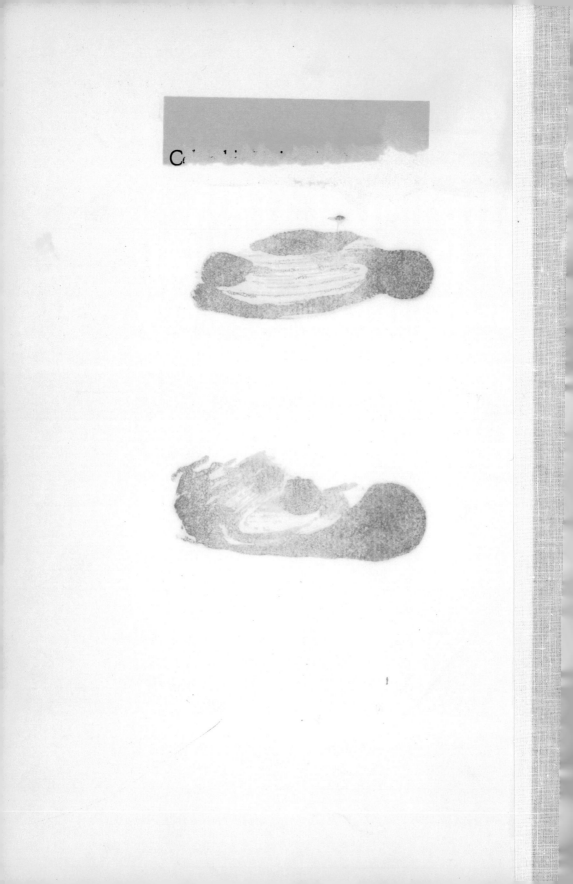

THE UNIFICATION OF ITALY, 1859–1861

THE UNIFICATION OF ITALY, 1859–1861

Cavour, Mazzini, or Garibaldi?

Edited by CHARLES F. DELZELL
Vanderbilt University

HOLT, RINEHART AND WINSTON
New York • Chicago • San Francisco • Toronto • London

Cover illustration (from left): Count Camillo Benso di Cavour, photograph (*Italian Cultural Institute*); Giuseppe Mazzini, photograph (*Italian Cultural Institute*); Giuseppe Garibaldi, from an engraving made after a photograph (*The Bettmann Archive*). Map on page vi by Dyno Lowenstein.

CONTENTS

BADEN BAVARIA

FRANCE

SWITZERLAND

AUSTRIAN EMPIRE

SAVOY

(1859)

LOMBARDY

VENETIA

Magenta
Novara • Solferino
Milan • Custoza
Villafranca

Venice

Turin

CEDED FROM
SARDINIA TO
FRANCE, 1860

PIEDMONT

PARMA

Po

TURKISH
EMPIRE

Genoa

MODENA

ROMAGNA

NICE
Nice

LIGURIAN
SEA

Florence
Arno River

MARCHES

Castelfidardo

TUSCANY

PAPAL STATES

UMBRIA

ADRIATIC SEA

CORSICA
(Fr.)

Tiber River

Rome

Pontecorvo

Caprera I.

Gaeta
Volturno River

Benevento

Naples

TYRRHENIAN
SEA

KINGDOM

SARDINIA

OF

Cagliari

Messina

Palermo

NAPLES

Marsala

SICILY

ITALY
1859-1860

KINGDOM OF SARDINIA

UNIFIED IN 1860

MEDITERRANEAN
SEA

0   50   100
Scale of Miles

INTRODUCTION

A little more than a century ago Italy emerged as a unified kingdom—in a process of liberal nationalist development that Italians like to call their *Risorgimento,* or "rebirth." Although historians disagree as to how early this process began, there can be no doubt that it reached its culmination between 1859 and 1861. The annexations of Venetia in 1866 and of Rome in 1870 were but epilogues.

General textbooks of European history sometimes give the impression that the romantic drama of the *Risorgimento* unfolded in a polite sequence of events. Giuseppe Mazzini, the austere prophet of a republican and centralized form of nationalism that must be the accomplishment of a popular uprising, was the first to walk on stage. After stirring his countrymen to their duties and opportunities and enjoying a moment of glory in 1849 as head of the short-lived Roman Republic, he faded pretty much from view. Next to appear was the hard-headed parliamentary liberal leader of Sardinia-Piedmont, Count Cavour, who after cleverly obtaining assistance from Emperor Napoleon III of France in 1859, stage-managed the rest of the drama. Most romantic of all was the swashbuckling ex-Mazzinian General Giuseppe Garibaldi, who brilliantly conquered Sicily and Naples in 1860 and then with self-effacing generosity handed them over to his sovereign, King Victor Emmanuel II of Sardinia-Piedmont, before retiring with a bag of seed corn to his islet of Caprera.

Anyone who has looked behind stage or read the controversial historical literature pertaining to the era knows that this is an oversimplification. The *Risorgimento* was not a drama in which the protagonists politely gave each other their cues and then quietly faded into the wings. Both Mazzini and Garibaldi lost little time in denouncing Cavour's newly unified state as a betrayal of all that they had been fighting for. And Napoleon III came to be cursed by many Italians for not doing more than he did. All sorts of disillusionment swept Italy after the poetry of the *Risorgimento* gave way to the prose of the post-*Risorgimento*. Deficiencies in the fragilely and hastily unified state gave rise to a whole series of polemics, and much blame came to be placed on those

1

Risorgimento leaders who willingly settled for less than a genuine social revolution.

In Italy (and to some extent elsewhere) historical interpretations of the *Risorgimento* have moved through successive phases. Initially it was customary for court historians to praise Cavour and the House of Savoy in almost eulogistic terms. But soon there emerged a backlash of sectional resentments against what was regarded as the excessive "Piedmontization" of Italy. Subsequently, the impact of the industrial revolution, the growth of democracy and of socialism, the dislocation produced by World War I, the ensuing destruction of the liberal state by Mussolini's Fascist regime, and the recent establishment of a republican form of government have all tended, in one way or another, to affect historical interpretations of the way in which Italy came to be unified.

Without too much oversimplification it can be said that at least four major historiographic tendencies now exist in Italy with respect to this subject. First, there is the liberal, anticlerical school that exalts Cavour's parliamentary regime and takes special interest in the ideas and activities of the political elite that emerged triumphant in the *Risorgimento*. Broadly speaking, this group reflects the influence of Benedetto Croce's neo-Hegelian, "idealist" school of history writing. For Croce, history was the rise and triumph of the liberal spirit. A second major current is represented by a rather socialistic and republican school, interested not only in political theories but also in the sociological and economic problems that tended to be ignored by the Croceans; this cluster has revived interest in the alternative approaches to unification espoused by Mazzini, Garibaldi, Carlo Cattaneo, and others. A third group are the twentieth-century communist writers who seek to interpret the *Risorgimento* within the fairly rigid Marxian terms of class struggle, but at the same time giving special attention to the problem of the peasantry who remained pretty much on the sidelines. Fourth, there is a new Catholic school of historians who hope to correct what they regard as excessively anticlerical interpretations by the other groups. Although foreign scholarship does not necessarily fit into these categories, one can distinguish between historians who look upon Cavour as the great hero of their story and those who give Garibaldi and Mazzini first honors.

This problem book focuses on several aspects of the broad question of who deserves credit for the unification of Italy between 1859 and 1861. The first section discusses whether unification was the result of design or of accident. More precisely, were Cavour and Napoleon III acting intentionally as architects of Italian unity? Do leaders shape the course of events, or do they merely respond to events beyond their control? In line with many earlier writers on the *Risorgimento,* Arthur J. Whyte, an English author of two volumes on

Cavour's life and letters, ascribes to Cavour great "clearness of vision," "anticipation of events," and a "sureness of touch" in all that he did from the time
he accepted a ministerial position in the Piedmontese government. From his
examination of Cavour's youthful correspondence, Whyte concludes that
Cavour even in his youth had high political ambitions and that he viewed the
Italian question as a single problem. In deciding whether Whyte is justified in
calling Cavour a "democrat," keep in mind the distinctions usually made in
midnineteenth-century Europe between "liberalism" and "democracy" (or
"radicalism," as it was often labeled on the Continent).

Some of Whyte's contenticns are questioned in the next selection by
L. C. B. Seaman, who has authored a thoughtful collection of "revisionist"
essays on European history. Seaman declares that Cavour was a parliamentary
liberal who did not believe in Italian unification because it was an idea tainted
with radicalism. He goes on to argue that Cavour "was always at great pains
to prove that everything that happened, happened because he had always
wanted it to happen and because his guiding genius was in complete control
from beginning to end." Yet in actual fact, Seaman continues, neither Cavour
nor Napoleon III wanted or expected Italian unification, and what took place
by 1861 occurred to a considerable degree in spite of them. Much of his case
turns on the geographical meaning to be given the term, "Kingdom of Italy."
In evaluating this argument one needs to determine what Cavour and Napoleon
agreed upon at their secret conference at Plombières in 1858.

The second section considers the role of Mazzinian republicanism in the
1850s and poses the question whether Mazzini's continuing stubborn insistence
on the need for a popular uprising and his opposition to any Napoleonic
intervention were a hindrance or a help to Italian unification. William Roscoe
Thayer insists categorically that Mazzini's activities in the 1850s were an anachronism and a hindrance to the cause of unity, in contrast to his constructive role
earlier in the century. Does Thayer show prejudice against the austere republican "prophet"?

An opposite appraisal of Mazzini's work in the 1850s is presented by Luigi
Salvatorelli, a distinguished Italian historian who has assumed an increasingly
outspoken democratic and republican position during the course of Italy's
vicissitudes in the twentieth century. Whereas Thayer contends that "if Piedmont had taken his [Mazzini's] advice after 1850, there would have been neither
independence nor unity," Salvatorelli argues that if it had not been for actions
taken by Mazzinians in the late 1850s, the events that produced unification
would not have occurred. For example, Felice Orsini's plot against Napoleon
III caused the latter to confer with Cavour at Plombières and to send an army
into the Po Valley in 1859 to help the Piedmontese drive the Austrians out of

Lombardy. Again, it was Mazzinianism that precipitated the insurrections in central Italy, Garibaldi's expedition to Sicily, and the Piedmontese intervention in the Marches and Umbria in 1860. Salvatorelli's essay has done much to stir modern historians to a re-evaluation of the role of Mazzinianism in this climactic period.

A somewhat different argument is offered by Adolfo Omodeo of Naples. Author of a scholarly but uncompleted biography of Cavour, he expresses admiration for both the Piedmontese statesman and Mazzini. He contends that Cavour was lucky to have Mazzini in opposition in 1859, because he could use him as a kind of political counterpoise and threat to dissuade the French from trying to impose their hegemony upon Italy. Thus Mazzini was by no means a negligible factor in 1859, and the slightest accident to Cavour might well have catapulted the republican once more into a position of leadership.

Probably the most heated historical debate of all revolves about Cavour's relationship with Garibaldi at the time of the latter's invasion of Sicily and Naples in 1860. Were Cavour and Garibaldi collaborators or rivals? The third section addresses this question. Cavour's problem of shaping a policy with respect to Garibaldi must be considered in light of the delicate international situation, which might be upset, and of the uncertain domestic political scene. For Cavour always had to ask himself how complete was Garibaldi's switch from Mazzinianism to support of King Victor Emmanuel II during the 1850s. Garibaldi clearly enjoyed strong support among democratic radicals in the new Action Party, a political grouping that stood somewhat to the left of Cavour's "moderate" liberals and included a good many people of former republican orientation. A vigorous defense of all Cavour's actions toward Garibaldi in this period is presented in a second selection from Thayer, his American biographer. Thayer emphasizes that the Premier never actually stopped Garibaldi from proceeding to Sicily; moreover, the connivance of Cavour's government was necessary for the expedition's success and was forthcoming.

In a counterargument on Cavour's attitude to the Sicilian expedition, Denis Mack Smith, an able British scholar who follows in the pro-Garibaldian tradition of George Macaulay Trevelyan, insists that "history is a great improviser" and that no simple formula will explain Cavour's attitude toward Garibaldi in May 1860. After marshaling various types of evidence, Mack Smith concludes that "far from helping Garibaldi while cleverly appearing not to (which is the traditional view), it seems that he gave no help while cleverly appearing as if he might do so at any moment." A second excerpt from Mack Smith comes from the concluding pages of *Cavour and Garibaldi, 1860,* his long monograph on the political struggle between Cavour and Garibaldi in the

months after the landing in Sicily. The thesis here is that "Cavour was sometimes treacherous, often uncertain, and always more or less hostile to Garibaldi;
and indeed one can almost say that he was *necessarily* all of these things."
What indeed were Cavour's preferences in 1860? What broad considerations
faced him as he watched Garibaldi's amazing conquest? Several Italian historians have charged that Mack Smith is quite unfair to Cavour. Do you find any
evidence of such bias?

Ettore Passerin d'Entrèves, a prominent Italian Catholic historian, provides a reply to Mack Smith. His account of Cavour's "last political battle"
in 1860–1861 rests on careful study of Cavour's recently published correspondence pertaining to the liberation of the south—material that Mack Smith also
had access to when he wrote *Cavour and Garibaldi, 1860*. Defending Cavour's
hasty dispatch of an army south to head off Garibaldi short of Rome, Passerin
d'Entrèves stresses both the international dangers that confronted Cavour and
the failure of Garibaldi to inaugurate a coherent administrative policy in
Naples. In view of Garibaldi's unrelenting military drive toward Rome and
Venetia, was it not better for Italy that he be stopped by other Italians and in
Italy, rather than by the almost inevitable European intervention that might
have put all in jeopardy and perhaps made of Italy another such place as
Hungary had become since 1849?

The legal procedure utilized to annex central and southern Italy is considered in the fourth section. Was it wise to use plebiscites, which restricted
the choice to a simple "yes" or "no"? Would it have been better to elect constituent assemblies and then negotiate with them the annexations on a more
or less equal basis? Contemplate the implications of the latter system—for
example, the possibility of the emergence of a decentralized federal structure
rather than the highly centralized Piedmontese system. In view of the hostility
of most of Garibaldi's entourage to Cavour's plebiscitary plan, why did Garibaldi finally accept it? To be sure, as George Macaulay Trevelyan observes in
the next selection, a solution by plebiscites could be reached faster in the midst
of a ticklish international situation than could a decision by constituent assemblies. Did this advantage, however, compensate for the frustrations felt by the
south at not being able to modify easily the Piedmontese constitution that was
being blanketed over Italy? Mack Smith contends that the plebiscitarian solution was a flaw in the original creation of the Italian state and that it led to
brigandage, instability, and the troublesome Southern Question. But did the
plebiscites really cause these things? Or did they merely aggravate deep-seated
problems?

In the next selection Seaman asks what the meaning was of the nearly
unanimous vote in the plebiscites. He argues that the center and the south

were not ready for unification and that Cavour's plebiscites proved only the negative proposition that the people were weary of the uncertainty that had prevailed since Garibaldi's first landing in Sicily and desired annexation as the only visible way of avoiding chaos. At best, the plebiscites were "a sort of emotional *te deum* proclaiming a general sense of thankfulness that the time of troubles was at an end." But were the regional troubles at an end? And to what extent was Garibaldi responsible for aggravating them?

Salvatorelli, author of the last excerpt in this section, agrees with many of the criticisms made of the plebiscites but observes that the new liberal regime provided the means for fitting the masses into the political and social life of the state—a point Mazzini refused to admit. Is Salvatorelli's thesis weakened by the fact that it was not until the eve of World War I that Italy achieved a really democratic franchise, and that it was not until after the disasters of Fascism and World War II that Italy replaced the original constitution with one that was more responsive to the needs of a complex modern society?

One of the thorniest problems of the *Risorgimento,* that of finding a compromise between the newly unified state and the papacy's doctrine of the temporal power (namely, the theory that the pope must possess territorial sovereignty in order to carry out his spiritual mission) is taken up in the fifth section. By early 1861 most of the Papal States had been wrenched away from Pius IX, but he still retained, with French support, the province around Rome. As most Italian nationalists were determined that Rome must eventually become the capital of the unified kingdom, Cavour suggested during the last months of his life the formula, "A free church in a free state," as a means of reconciling the papacy with the Italian kingdom. What precisely did this formula imply? With the help of certain intermediaries, more or less serious negotiations went on for a time between Turin and Rome. Suddenly the talks came to an end. Who was to blame? According to Thayer, Cavour's staunchly Protestant biographer, the Jesuits torpedoed the negotiations. Quite a different conclusion is drawn by the English-born Catholic historian, Edward E. Y. Hales. He concedes that what Cavour offered the Church was generous by contemporary Piedmontese and French standards and that Cavour's program did have a chance of success because it was based on a principle, substituting for the temporal power superior spiritual advantages for the Church. The pope failed to agree because of the glaring contrast between Cavour's "fair words and his government's ruthless actions." Which writer has the most evidence at his disposal?

The last section of the book centers on evaluation of the *Risorgimento* in retrospect. Benedetto Croce proudly declares that it was a historical masterpiece of liberal nationalism which offered an admirable example to other peoples. Numerous other commentators have insisted, however, that the *Risorgimento* was a historical inadequacy—that somehow it fell short of what it should have been. Raymond Grew takes this stand and argues that the Cavourian moderates needlessly sacrificed opportunities for structural reforms and political education of the masses. To what extent can the historian properly criticize the past for not unfolding differently from the way it did?

One of the noteworthy developments in recent Italian historiography has been the emergence of an outspokenly communist school. Its writers have sought to take over the study of economic and social history—partly by default of the Crocean school, which traditionally has disdained "material" aspects of the past. Their interpretations of the *Risorgimento* derive chiefly from the notes that were stealthily jotted down in a Fascist prison by Antonio Gramsci, founder of the Italian Communist Party and its leader until his death in 1937. The "Gramsci thesis" criticizes the Mazzinian-Garibaldian wing of the *Risorgimento* for not extending the revolutionary movement into the countryside in the way the Jacobins did during the French Revolution. Whereas the latter, by means of a skillful agrarian policy, made rural France accept the leadership of Paris, the Italian Action Party failed to follow their example. The victory of the *Risorgimento* took place without a concomitant winning of the support of the peasant masses through a clear-cut democratic ideology and an agrarian reform program. Thus, according to Gramsci, the *Risorgimento* did not develop into a real revolution; instead it was an agrarian *rivoluzione mancata* (that is, a revolutionary opportunity that was muffed—what the French would call a *révolution manquée*). Such an agrarian revolution, it is argued, would by raising the standard of living among the peasantry have guaranteed a wider market to urban industry and allowed a greater industrial development than actually occurred. Is Gramsci justified in making these comparisons between Italy and France? Did the Jacobin experience offer an infallible model for Italy? And is there any truth to Gramsci's assertion that Cavour really controlled the Action Party?

The underlying question of whether Italy was ripe for an agrarian revolution in 1860 is considered by Rosario Romeo, a Crocean liberal and capitalist historian who has seen fit to move into the field of economic and social history. In his *Risorgimento e capitalismo* Romeo seeks to refute the Gramsci thesis. "Objective" conditions for an agrarian revolution simply did not exist in 1860, he insists. Furthermore, the absence of agrarian revolution did not really delay industrialization. Gramsci's reflections about the absence of collaboration between the bourgeoisie and the peasants in the *Risorgimento* were based on the practical political experience of communists when they sought to win peasant support in the strife-torn years after World War I. They are, therefore, not valid historical criteria for the 1860 situation.

In the light of the divergent interpretations presented in this book, what verdict can be rendered to the overall questions posed? Who advanced, who hindered the unification of Italy between 1859 and 1861? What is the significance of the *Risorgimento* in retrospect? Was it a masterpiece of liberal nationalism or a *rivoluzione mancata*? May we hope to reach agreement in an evaluation of the *Risorgimento* and its protagonists? Or must we reconcile ourselves to the dictum expressed by the Dutch scholar, Pieter Geyl, after long study of oscillating interpretations of Napoleon I, that history is "argument without end"?

THE HISTORIANS CLASH

Unification: By design or force of circumstances?
"Italy found in Cavour one who . . . viewed Italy and the Italian question as a single problem, and thus lifted the whole complex controversy from the lower level of a mere redistribution of Italian soil (as Napoleon III and others regarded it) on to the higher plane of the creation of a nation."—Arthur J. Whyte.

"Cavour did not, like Mazzini and Garibaldi, believe in Italian unification. For him the idea was tainted with Radicalism, and his diplomat's sense of realities told him there were too many insurmountable obstacles in the way. All these factors in his political character made him acceptable to Napoleon III who likewise was not planning the unification of Italy."—L. C. B. Seaman.

Mazzinianism: Hindrance or help to unification?
"If Piedmont had taken [Mazzini's] advice after 1850, there would have been neither independence nor unity."—William Roscoe Thayer.

"The Plombières meeting . . . provides the true point of departure for 1859 —that is, the period in which the Italian political *Risorgimento* was achieved. It is not a case of direct continuity from the Crimean War and the Congress of Paris [1856] but rather of a new start—a start by Napoleon III, but undertaken because of the decisive influence of the Action Party and Mazzini."—Luigi Salvatorelli.

"Unification of Italy required that somebody during the crisis of 1859 assume the unpopular stance that Mazzini had to take. . . . The threat of Mazzinianism served to precipitate both . . . Napoleon and . . . Vienna into war; and, at the same time, the exile without a following served to limit and check the French plan of action in Italy."—Adolfo Omodeo.

9

Cavour and Garibaldi: Collaborators or rivals?

"Had it depended on Garibaldi alone, the [Sicilian] expedition would never have started; without Garibaldi, it could never have started. . . . Equally necessary was the connivance of the Government."—William Roscoe Thayer.

"The conclusion then must be that Cavour played a less important and less happy part than often thought in the movement which conquered half Italy from the Bourbons. The facts only fit together if we assume, first, that there was a kind of hiatus in his policy; and secondly, that on balance he did more initially to hinder than to help the conquest of Sicily. . . .

"Cavour was sometimes treacherous, often uncertain, and always more or less hostile to Garibaldi; and indeed one can almost say that he was *necessarily* all of these things."—Denis Mack Smith.

"Consciously or otherwise, Mack Smith underestimates an entire series of testimonies which tend to confirm the coherency and the *logicality* of Cavour's policy, despite all its changeableness, during the summer of 1860. He has made his own personal selection from the documents and has deliberately excluded those that might negate his . . . interpretation."—Ettore Passerin d'Entrèves.

Cavour's use of plebiscites: Desirable or regrettable?

"If Italy had had no armed enemies to fear either within or without the barrier of her guardian Alps, if she had been in safe possession of her own house, then indeed she ought to have gone about the difficult business of setting it in order with long and careful deliberation. . . . [But] that autumn . . . it would have been the height of unwisdom to waste two months in electing and calling together Neapolitan and Sicilian assemblies, and half a year more in bargainings and intrigues of every kind, public and personal."—George Macaulay Trevelyan.

"The limitations and incompleteness of [the victory of the plebiscite] were to be of great importance. . . . Not only did they bear directly on the emergence of a 'southern question' in Italian politics, but neither the radicals nor the regionalists were ever quite reconciled to finding the fruit of their labours plucked by other people. The tensions set up between the various regions and political parties were never to be properly resolved."—Denis Mack Smith.

"The centre and south were not ready for unification, and the plebiscites in favour of annexation to the house of Savoy proved only certain negative propositions."—L. C. B. Seaman.

"A major consequence of this 'construction out of necessity' . . . was that the common people, because they had not participated directly in the construction [of the state], could not even make it take cognizance of their interests. . . . Nevertheless, for this . . . deficiency . . . the possibility of remedial action existed within the liberal regime."—Luigi Salvatorelli.

Cavour and Pius IX: "A free church in a free state"

"In a burst of pontifical fury Cavour's attempt to harmonize Church and State in Italy [came to an end]. . . . The underlying obstacle was the astuteness with which the Curia, composed almost wholly of Italians, used the doctrine of the Temporal Power to serve their own ends and to perpetuate the preponderance of the Italians in the hierarchy."—William Roscoe Thayer.

"Why, then, did the negotiations fail? . . . The reason lies in the glaring contrast between Cavour's fair words and his government's ruthless actions."—Edward E. Y. Hales.

The *Risorgimento* in retrospect

"If it were possible in political history to speak of masterpieces as we do in dealing with works of art, the process of Italy's independence, liberty, and unity would deserve to be called the masterpiece of the liberal-national movements of the nineteenth century."—Benedetto Croce.

"The way in which Italy was united left a dull, persistent ache in the Italian body politic. . . . The feeling of the revolution *manquée* was born with the successes of 1859."—Raymond Grew.

"In order to counter the moderates effectively, it is evident that the Action Party should have attached itself to the rural masses, especially in the south. It should have been 'Jacobin' not only in external 'form' and temperament, but above all in its economic and social program."—Antonio Gramsci.

"Two basic questions should be raised with respect to the Gramsci thesis. The first relates to the real possibility of an agrarian revolution, to the actual existence, in other words, of an alternative course of action to that which the *Risorgimento* pursued. The second relates to the question whether such an alternative course would have produced an outcome somewhat more progressive than what actually resulted."—Rosario Romeo.

The late ARTHUR J. WHYTE, an English scholar, published between 1925 and 1930 a sympathetic two-volume study of the life and letters of Count Cavour, whom he called the "architect of Italian unity." Basing his account on the correspondence of Cavour that was then available and on the classic biography written just before World War I by the liberal Senator Francesco Ruffini of Italy, Whyte made it clear that in his opinion Cavour even in his youth had high political ambitions and viewed the Italian question as a single problem.*

Cavour: Architect of Unity

Cavour is known in history as the architect of the modern Kingdom of Italy. When he was nominated First Minister of King Victor Emmanuel II of Sardinia in 1852, Italy was divided into eight separate states—the Kingdoms of Sardinia and Naples, the States of the Church, the Grand Duchy of Tuscany, and the Duchies of Modena, Parma, and Lucca, with Venetia and Lombardy as Provinces of the Austrian Empire. Italy thus divided was the work of the Congress of Vienna in 1815, and represented the latest redistribution of her soil in a series whose permutations and combinations had prevented the unity of Italy

for a thousand years. When Cavour died in 1861 Italy was a single kingdom under Victor Emmanuel, save for Venetia and the city of Rome.

It was Cavour who by wise domestic policy first won the respect and confidence of Europe, and later by a bold and hazardous statesmanship sent the flower of the little Sardinian army to the aid of France and England in the Crimea, raising the prestige of Italy and earning the gratitude of the Western Powers. It was Cavour who pilloried Austria in the eyes of Europe at the Congress of Paris and knew how to utilise the defeat of Russia to wean England from her tra-

---

    * From Arthur J. Whyte, *The Early Life and Letters of Cavour, 1810-1848* (London: Oxford University Press, 1925), pp. xi-xviii. Reprinted by permission of the Clarendon Press, Oxford.

ditional alliance with Austria to become the warm supporter of Italian freedom. Finally, it was the same clear brain and firm hand which brought Napoleon III into Italy in 1859, broke the power of Austria and kept Italy free from foreign interference while Garibaldi won the Kingdom of Naples for Italy and Victor Emmanuel.

This great work of Cavour's has been widely written upon . . . But Cavour as a man, apart from a statesman, is not as well known as his work. In all that he did from the moment that he accepted office as Minister of Commerce and Agriculture, there was a clearness of vision and a sureness of touch which indicated the master hand. There was no hint of indecision, weakness or lack of experience in his work, but a maturity of judgment and a fulness of knowledge which could only have come from a long and arduous apprenticeship. . . . [His is a] story of the making of a statesman through long years of patient waiting and unceasing preparation. . . .

The early life of a great statesman may or may not be of genuine interest. But the life of any man who sets before himself in youth a high ambition, and in spite of almost insuperable difficulties achieves it, must always be instructive and worthy of attention. Such in a sentence was the early life of Cavour. Almost from childhood he was obsessed with political ambition. At the age of fifteen he startled his worthy professor of mathematics, who sought to stimulate his ability for figures by the prospect of becoming a famous mathematician, by replying, 'This is not the time for mathematics; one must study economies; the world progresses. I hope to see the day when our country has a constitution,

and who knows but I may be a minister in it.' To this dictum he steadily adhered and in his fortieth year he saw its fulfilment.

. . . The years from Cavour's birth in 1810 to his entrance into Parliament in 1848 [were] a period during which two great movements were in progress, the industrial revolution and the rise of democracy. The general political condition of Europe during this period cannot be better described than by a simile drawn from the story of Watt and the kettle, in which the new industrial democracy is the heated water seeking expansion but kept firmly down by the lid of autocracy —represented by the policy of the Holy Alliance—whilst the boss on the lid took the form of the grim figure of Prince Metternich. The kettle boiled over in 1848.

If we omit the years of Cavour's boyhood, this period corresponds almost exactly to the reigns of Louis Philippe in France and Charles Albert of Savoy in Italy, and to the era of the Reform Bill and the Corn Law agitation in England. Industrially, it was the period which saw the application of steam to transport in the form of railways and steamships, and to industry in the rise of modern machinery. The birth of modern banking, the application of machinery to agriculture, the use of gas for street lighting, and many other inventions and developments date from this same epoch.

Cavour was the child of his age. Though the son of aristocratic and royalist parents, held at the font by a sister of Napoleon and named, suggestively enough, Camillo, after his godfather Prince Borghese, he was born a democrat. From his father he inherited a strong will and an aptitude for business, and from his mother, a Swiss of Huguenot ancestry, his love of freedom and his democratic leanings. The tenacity of his democratic ideas and his imprudence in advocating them ruined the military career designed for him by his father and put him in chronic opposition to his family, his social circle, and the court. Debarred in consequence from the one career he desired, he adopted a business life. Beginning with agriculture, he was soon immersed in schemes for railways, mills, steamboats, banks, and other ventures, some of which failed and some of which succeeded, but which all brought him knowledge and experience. In spite of his multifarious business activities he found time to write a series of very able articles on social and economic subjects, and was rapidly making a name for himself as a writer, when the Piedmontese reforms of 1847 sent him into journalism as editor of his own paper, *Il Risorgimento* (The Resurrection). It was from this position that he passed in June, 1848, to a seat in the Chamber of Deputies.

During these years Cavour continually widened his horizon both by study and travel. Always a student, he read either in French, Italian, or English all the standard works on history, political philosophy, economics and agriculture that he could obtain. In his numerous sojourns in Paris and his two visits to England he made a close study of the political, industrial and social conditions of both countries. To this was added an intimate knowledge of Switzerland and a close relationship with many of the best known thinkers and politicians both in this latter country and in France. Both in Geneva and Paris he attended university lectures and, in short, there were few avenues of political and social informa-

tion, apart from practical experience, which Cavour had not done his best to explore before his political life began.

Soon after 1830 Cavour's political principles began to crystallise, and two years later he had adopted that attitude of the *juste milieu* to which he remained faithful throughout his life. This midway position, which condemned equally the reactionary tendencies of the Royalists and the revolutionary propaganda of the Socialists, and which he described later as moderate-Liberal, commended him neither to the Conservatives nor the Republicans, each of whom believed him to belong to the opposite party, and his principles did not materialise into an active force until his famous *connubio*[1] with the Left-Centre under Ratazzi in 1852.

The materials available for the reconstruction of Cavour's life before his entrance into politics consist of some hundreds of letters, his diary and published articles, and, for the first six months of 1848, his leaders in *Il Risorgimento*. The letters are evenly distributed and enable us to follow his activities steadily year by year with scarcely a break. The personal portrait which emerges from the letters is a pleasant one. This first movement of Cavour's life might well be headed 'allegro con brio.' His sense of humour, his unceasing activity, his unfailing interest in intellectual pursuits, together with his affection for his family and his concern for them in sickness and trouble, reveals a happy and attractive nature. Intellectually precocious, he had all the omniscience of youth, and in his early years the lectures he delivered to his correspondents caused frequent irri-

[1] A political alliance (marriage) with the left of center liberals.—*Ed.*

tation. His home life from his eighteenth to his thirtieth year, however, was very often far from happy. His father was engrossed in business. His mother and her two sisters divided their attention between throne and altar, and his brother was immersed in philosophy and the care of his own family. The palazzo at Turin was the happy hunting-ground of ultramontane clerics and extreme reactionaries. Politics were taboo and business was despised. To fill in his time Cavour gambled and lost more than he could afford, and got mixed up in social intrigues and love affairs which he thought were more serious than they were. The dull social life of Turin, 'half barrack and half monastery,' disgusted him. He had neither money nor status and was generally looked askance at as a Liberal of unknown iniquity. But the moment he got away from Turin to Paris or to his cousins at Geneva he became another being. In the big world outside, where he could speak his mind with freedom, he was as cheerful and interested as he was bored and miserable at home.

Many of his later letters are concerned entirely with business, either agriculture, stock-raising, or industrial undertakings in which he was interested. . . . In these, his grasp of detail, his power of generalisation and width of outlook are very noticeable. The remaining letters are chiefly political and are concerned mainly with France and England. They reveal an understanding not only of internal and external problems but of the trend of political currents very unusual in a stranger. His forecasts of political movements are often very accurate and his anticipation of events sometimes remarkable.

A noticeable feature of his correspondence is the absence of allusions to Italian or Austrian politics. This, no doubt, was due partly to prudence and the extreme severity of the censorship, but partly also to Cavour's attitude towards the entire system of absolutism. As a matter of fact the political life of Italy during these years was dull. The periodic outbreaks fomented by Mazzini were more symptomatic than dangerous and resembled the uprising of bad gasses upon the surface of a stagnant pool. Cavour regarded all the Italian governments as part and parcel of a system which already belonged to the past, irksome and vicious, and doomed to be presently superseded by the new order of things arising in the West. He was not in the least interested in domestic politics and was only too pleased if he could get away to France or Switzerland and breathe a freer air. In this fact lay much of Cavour's success as a statesman. He belonged to the new order. He turned his face to the future and steadily refused to look back. Consciously or unconsciously his policy was that of his people. He had caught the spirit of the new age: its sense of nationality, its thirst for material progress, and its desire for self-government. Whatever might be said against him, he could never be justly accused of sympathy with the system of absolutism.

Taking these letters as a whole, what strikes us most perhaps is the width and range of Cavour's interests. He had little leaning towards art and polite letters, but with these exceptions there was hardly a branch of knowledge which did not interest him. The world of politics, from foreign policy and the growth and interaction of parties down to details of procedure and methods of election; industry, from the movements of foreign trade to the latest inventions and improvements in machinery; chemistry and science; social reform; education; economics and agriculture;—in all of these his interest was perennial. No text-books were too dull, no blue-books too dry, to quench his enthusiasm. Scarcely less astonishing than the range of his interests was his mental and physical energy. He was capable of working at the highest pressure for weeks and even months on end. Sleep and recreation he reduced to a minimum. He was indeed, as d'Azeglio said of him, 'd'une activité diabolique.'[2] With this tremendous vitality he combined extraordinary thoroughness. His power of concentration was remarkable. His memory was prodigious. To this equipment he added courage, self-confidence, and readiness to take responsibility. He was no idealist but a practical opportunist. Early in life he wrote down in his diary a motto to which he adhered steadily all his life: 'Pour être un homme d'Etat utile, il faut avant tout avoir le *tact* des choses possibles.'[3]

With the eye of the true statesman he saw that the future prosperity of his country depended on its power to assimilate the movements of the age, and as a pioneer in the application of science to industry and an advocate of constitutional government he did his best to promote the true interests of his country. A warm admirer of England, of whose statesmen Pitt, Canning and Peel were his models, he would gladly, when the time came, have broken away from the bureaucratic and centralised system inherited from France in favour of the more free and independent methods of England, but the constitution was made without him. A convinced free trader, he rejoiced over the abolition of the Corn Laws, though he was deceived in his opinion that the rest of Europe must of necessity follow the example set by England. He understood the value of public opinion in this country and was more anxious to obtain the good word of the Press than the commendation of individual statesmen, an attitude he reversed when dealing with France.

In conclusion, we cannot read this record of Cavour's pre-political life without being impressed by the peculiar fitness of his training for the rôle he was to play a few years later. At the moment when the old absolutist system was passing away, it gave Piedmont a statesman not only entirely sympathetic with the new régime of constitutionalism, but one who had studied it deeply and carefully in the countries where it was most successful. And moreover one who, having been kept entirely apart from the previous form of government, had neither old habits to unlearn nor new ones to acquire. Again, at the moment when the future prosperity of the country required the adoption of the new means and methods revealed by the industrial revolution, it put at the head of the government a business man and a financier, who in all matters relating to industry was a pioneer and a modernist. Lastly, in the wider sphere of international relations, at the very moment when the sense of nationality was becoming the keynote of European politics, Italy found in Cavour one who, as Gioberti said, 'made the mistake' of governing a small country as if it was an empire; a man who, uninfluenced by the squabbles and jealousies of the vari-

[2] Devilishly active.—*Ed.*
[3] "To be a useful statesman, one must have a feeling for what is feasible."—*Ed.*

ous Italian states, viewed Italy and the Italian question as a single problem, and thus lifted the whole complex controversy from the lower level of a mere redistribution of Italian soil (as Napoleon III and others regarded it) on to the higher plane of the creation of a nation. He stepped into public life at the darkest hour of his country's history and by sheer ability, courage, and faith forced her to place her destiny in his hands.

The excerpt that follows comes from a collection of rather unorthodox interpretations of nineteenth-century European history by L. C. B. SEAMAN, a young Cambridge-trained English schoolmaster. In effect he disputes some of the views set forth by Whyte in the previous selection. According to Seaman, neither Cavour nor Napoleon III wanted or expected Italian unification. Their actions were not carefully pre-meditated and they thought only of northern Italy. Whatever one thinks about Seaman's conclusions, there can be no complaint about any dullness of style.*

Cavour and Napoleon III: Instruments of Destiny

The starting point of a rational understanding of events in Italy between 1858 and 1861 is a realization that in 1858 neither Napoleon III nor Cavour wanted or expected Italian unification. The achievement, by 1861, of an Italian kingdom comprising the whole of peninsular Italy except Rome, was something which though it happened partly because of Napoleon III and Cavour, happened to a considerable degree in spite of both of them.

The first confusion arises out of the meaning of the words 'Kingdom of Italy.' To all who consider the phrase after 1861 it obviously means the area ruled over by Victor Emmanuel from that year onwards, an area felt to be incomplete because it did not at that date already include either Rome or Venetia. But this is not what the phrase 'Kingdom of Italy' meant before 1861. Its meaning is best elicited by examining a map of Europe either in the heyday of Napoleon I or in the time of Charlemagne. It is at once clear that the establishment of a King-dom of Italy, so far from involving the unification of the entire peninsula under one sovereignty could, on the basis of the medieval and the Napoleonic herit-

* From L. C. B. Seaman, *From Vienna to Versailles* (New York: Coward-McCann, Inc., 1956), pp. 69–78, 91–92, 94–95. Copyright 1956 by Coward-McCann, Inc. Reprinted by permission of Coward-McCann, Inc., New York, and Methuen & Co. Ltd., London.

age, be applied only to some variously defined part of northern Italy.

It is certain therefore that Napoleon III's phrase about 'doing something for Italy' was even vaguer than it looks, for the word 'Italy' was susceptible of various interpretations. It is safe to assume that the Emperor's famous words were not intended to involve anything much more than the expulsion of the Austrians from the northern part of Italy; that they involved the idea of 'freedom' only in a highly qualified sense; and that they did not at all involve Italy's unification.

The creation of an Italian kingdom was, as it turned out, contrary to the interests of France. So also, as it turned out, was the creation of a German Empire. The dominating position of France in Europe in the past had depended on the weakness of both Italy and Germany. Nor was Napoleon III stupid enough to desire either of them to come into existence in the shapes they actually assumed. He seems to have wanted to do in Italy and Germany what Napoleon I had done—to create large French client states in those areas, and at the same time, though this was not essential, to acquire additional territory for France. The scheme had the additional advantage that in both areas the achievement of this policy would result in a diminution of the power and prestige of the Habsburgs who stood for the dynastic principle, of which Napoleon was Europe's chief public opponent.

It is therefore incorrect to think of Napoleon III as venturing into Italy because he was blinded by a romantic attachment to the cause of Italian nationalism. He took the action he did because he thought it was compatible with the extension of French influence in Italy. In doing something for Italy he would

do something for France as well, and perhaps, if he could, something for the Bonapartes also. On the other hand it is wrong to think of his intervention as purely a matter of Machiavellian subtlety that misfired. The Man of December was far too much a product of his age not to share sincerely the contemporary dream of a free and regenerate Italy; and his entirely personal decision to take the first decisive move whence sprang the creation of an independent Italy has usually been treated with scant justice.

For in taking the step he did he was behaving in conformity both with the Napoleonic tradition and the Napoleonic legend. The voice from St Helena told him that the first monarch to espouse the cause of the 'peoples' would become the undisputed leader of Europe. That he should intervene to deliver the Italians from the Austrians was consistent with his self-chosen role as leader of the nationalities; and he clearly felt that in so doing he was placing France and himself at the head of the most powerful political force of the day. He and France, by co-operating with history, could secure the mastery of Europe's destiny by a great act of moral leadership which was also a piece of shrewd international statecraft.

Intervention was facilitated by the circumstance that it was Cavour with whom he had to deal. Alone among continental Liberals Cavour clearly understood the problem of power and that it could be solved solely by using the apparatus of power-politics, diplomacy and war. It was for this reason that he saw to it that Piedmont came to acquire this essential apparatus. He himself supplied the diplomacy, and the Piedmontese, often against their will, provided the armies and paid for their armament. But since the resources of Piedmont were small it was necessary to compensate for this fact by diplomacy of exceptional subtlety. Only by great skill would it be possible to secure the support of a Great Power and yet retain a reasonable measure of genuine independence for Piedmont; as it was, Cavour was widely accused of being Napoleon III's lackey and he was in fact far more sensitive to the need to placate the Emperor than is sometimes realized by those who are over-hasty to believe that Cavour was not merely an able man but a super-man.

Because he understood power-politics, Cavour was not a revolutionary. His spiritual home was remote indeed from the terrestrial paradise of regenerate nations linked together in brotherly love that Mazzini's mind habitually dwelt in; and Cavour hardly belonged to the same universe as Garibaldi, moving with the manly directness of a fighting pioneer from one camp fire to another. Cavour was a Liberal in the style of the July Monarchy, and had he been as French as his critics sometimes said he was, it would have been Cavour rather than Thiers or Guizot who would have guided the destinies of Orleanist France and have made a very much better job of it. Indeed there were times when his methods of managing the Parliament at Turin resembled those of Guizot more closely than those of Sir Robert Peel. As a Parliamentary Liberal, too, Cavour did not, like Mazzini and Garibaldi, believe in Italian unification. For him the idea was tainted with Radicalism, and his diplomat's sense of realities told him there were too many insurmountable obstacles in the way.

All these factors in his political character made him acceptable to Napoleon III who likewise was not planning the unification of Italy and could not prejudice his position by association with Radical insurrectionaries. In short, Cavour made the Italian movement respectable and safe. Or so it seemed.

Whatever else was planned at Plombières it was therefore not Italian unification. It appears that Napoleon III's plans were always fluid and the programme agreed on was always subject to variation in the Emperor's mind. A reasonable scheme would, he thought, involve the expulsion of Austrian influence from north and centre and the reform of the various systems of government elsewhere in Italy. Lombardy-Venetia, the Duchies and perhaps the Romagna, could be added to Sardinia to make a Kingdom of Italy large enough to be a useful French client-state but not powerful enough to resist the cession of Savoy (and Nice perhaps) or to pursue a genuinely independent policy of its own. Alternatively, Tuscany and the Romagna could form a second client state under the rule of somebody capable of substituting French for Austrian influence—perhaps the Emperor's cousin, Prince Napoleon. The Two Sicilies could perhaps be persuaded to become yet another French client state by replacing the unpopular Bourbons by Murat, yet another of the Emperor's cousins. The Pope would (somehow) be persuaded to acquiesce in the whole process by being made President of an Italian Federation to which the new Italian states would all dutifully adhere. All of the various interests concerned would then be satisfied—Italian patriots by the expulsion of the Austrians; Liberals by the abolition of ancient misgovernment; Victor Emmanuel and Cavour by the greatly increased size and prestige of Piedmont; the French clericals by the new dignity of the Pope; the French patriots by the acquisition of new territory and by the substitution of French for Austrian influence throughout the length and breadth of Italy; and the Bonapartes by the creation of new family connections in Italy.

One version of this never definitively formulated programme was offered Cavour at Plombières, another was actually agreed on there, and the last and most modest version emerged at Villafranca. Many of the variations upon it were no more than suggestions whispered into the ears of slightly bewildered ambassadors and those unofficial contact-men of all nationalities for whom the Emperor had such a great weakness.

As for what Cavour had in mind in his dealings with Napoleon III, it is probable that he was not fundamentally more precise and fixed in his objectives than the Emperor. The greatness of Cavour is like the greatness of Bismarck in this respect; it consists not in the undeviating pursuit of a ruthless master plan concocted in advance of events, but rather in the infinite suppleness with which he adapted his policy and his objectives to every changing circumstance yet at the same time remaining firmly in control. His famous sense of what was possible consisted precisely in being able to see clearly what was possible at each given moment. It is the ability to control a situation that is constantly fluid that marks the able statesman; and the success of Cavour and Bismarck is due to their possessing this ability, just as Napoleon III's inability to do so was a major cause of his failure.

All that can safely be said is that Cavour wanted to get as much as could reasonably be obtained, but no more. He certainly envisaged the acquisition of Tuscany and the Romagna, and although his great triumph at Plombières was to get Napoleon to agree to Piedmont acquiring the Romagna, he seems to have played the Emperor false about Tuscany. But his acquiescence in the proposal to cede Savoy and possibly Nice indicates how very far indeed Cavour was from being the apostle of Italian Nationalism as such. Cavour was far more concerned, and far more fitted, to play the role of an international diplomat than that of the instrument of popular Nationalism. Plombières thus only looked like a demagogic plot. In reality it was much more like an old-fashioned piece of eighteenth century diplomacy on traditional horse-dealing lines. Phrases such as 'the cradle of the dynasty' or 'the sacred soil of the fatherland' had no place in Cavour's vocabulary. If the Duchies and the Romagna were only to be had by giving up Savoy and Nice, then Savoy and Nice would have to be given up, and principles would have to give way to necessity.

Thus, it may well be that there was after all not much more deception involved in Cavour's treatment of Napoleon III than there was in Bismarck's treatment of the Emperor at Biarritz. And because no Italian federation resulted from Plombières, that does not mean that Cavour necessarily disliked that idea, either. True, if such a federation were to emerge, Cavour envisaged Piedmont as its effectual head rather than the Pope; but whereas a federation in Italy seemed a reasonable possibility, a unitary Italy did not, in 1858. And

Cavour was not interested in the impossible. It is necessary to beware of Cavour's readiness to falsify the record after the event in the interests of his own reputation. Like Bismarck he was always at great pains to prove that everything that happened, happened because he had always wanted it to happen and because his guiding genius was in complete control of affairs from beginning to end. But that does not mean that he is to be believed when he says this, any more than Bismarck is to be believed when he says the same sort of thing about the creation of the German Empire.

The fact is that both the men of Plombières were deceived—by the Italians in general and by Garibaldi in particular. It was not merely Napoleon III's careful schemes which were swept away by Italian revolutionary zeal; Cavour's nice diplomatic calculations went the same way too. One thing about the Plombières agreement is certain; it is that neither of the two men who made it dreamed that they were inaugurating a series of events that in three years would make Victor Emmanuel king over all Italy.

As soon as the Emperor began, in his serpentine way, to prepare French and European opinion for his coming intervention in Italy, he quickly came to the conclusion that he had blundered into a trap of his own making. A man as meditative and as impressionable as he was could not fail to see how difficult it was going to be to limit and control the passions his intervention would inevitably arouse: the heady patriotism of Italian Liberals and Radicals, the justifiable fears of Catholics everywhere at this gratuitous patronage of the most belligerently anti-clerical government in Europe, and above all the furious determination of Cavour himself. Consequently it is possible to see reason in Napoleon's vacillations after Plombières. Right up to the moment of the agreement at Villafranca he devoted as much ingenuity to trying to get out of the trap he had fallen into as Cavour did in trying to keep him in it. As it was Napoleon all but succeeded in escaping; and was on the very brink of salvation when he was pushed back into the clutches of Cavour by the despatch of the fatal Austrian ultimatum. For when it arrived Cavour was about to accept the scheme for the demobilization of all the three Powers which had been proposed by the British and apparently accepted by the Austrians as well as the French. After that the Emperor had no alternative but to march into the hornets' nest, driven to it by the unscrupulousness of Cavour and the folly of the Habsburgs.

Despite the rashness of his utterances in Milan after Magenta when he appeared publicly to give 'the Italians' *carte blanche* to do what they liked, Villafranca was not a real reversal of Napoleon's policy, and not, even in its failure to liberate Venetia, a betrayal of the cause of Italy, if the phrase is intended to imply the unification of the entire country, for this had never been in question. Napoleon was certainly going back on his agreement with Cavour and on his promises made in Milan. But it ill became Cavour, of all people, to complain if, after the shambles at Magenta and Solferino, and with all Europe and half France hostile to him, Napoleon felt no longer able to fight Cavour's battles for him. If the Villafranca proposals dissatisfied the Piedmontese, they secured for them more than they could have got if Napoleon had stayed at home. Piedmont obtained Lombardy and Parma. Napoleon III gained nothing; not Nice, to which he had little claim, nor even Savoy, to which he had, on national grounds at any rate, at least as good a claim as Piedmont had to Romagna and the Duchies. Indeed, the really humiliating thing about Villafranca was that it represented failure for Cavour. Against the insistence of the Radicals that Italy should and could liberate herself by her own unaided efforts, Cavour had asserted the superiority of the orthodox methods of diplomacy and war in association with Napoleon III. And unlike Napoleon III, Cavour could resign after Villafranca, and thus appear to dissociate himself from what was after all the collapse of the policy on which he had staked his whole claim to be the leader of the Risorgimento. His rage is understandable; but in flouncing out of office he was not merely giving vent to his feelings. He was also pulling out on the partner he had himself chosen, leaving him to bear the stigma of treachery while preserving for himself the reputation of an outraged and bitterly disappointed patriot.

Moreover, though Cavour was out of office, Ricasoli in Tuscany, Farini in Modena and D'Azeglio in the Romagna had been, and remained, busily at work on his behalf, ensuring that in all three places the movement for annexation to Piedmont should triumph over all obstacles and silence every criticism. The Villafranca proposals to return all three areas to their legitimate rulers threatened to stultify their work. Yet the fact that these regions did not so revert was as much the result of the decisions of Napoleon III as the annexation of Lombardy and Parma. Cavour in fact went on negotiating with the traitor of Villa-franca, and through those negotiations got the Duchies and the Romagna after all, and, what is more, Cavour insisted that the traitor got his price—Savoy and Nice.

If the cession of Savoy and Nice lost Cavour much prestige in Italy, it was a step which cost Napoleon III a good deal more. It wrecked his own proposal for a Congress to settle the Italian problem, because no Congress would ever give him Savoy and Nice, and the change of front increased his reputation for double-dealing and made him appear greedy for territory, which in fact he was not. It made nonsense of his appeal to the principle of nationality since he had no national claim to Nice. He could claim it only on the grounds that with Savoy it helped to adjust the balance of power in the interests of France; but the popular side of his prestige was based on the assumption that he, alone among the rulers of Europe, stood, not for the balance of power, but for the principle of nationality. The annexation also prevented his obtaining the renewal of English friendship he had sought by at last openly abandoning the Pope in the pamphlet 'The Pope and the Congress'; in this he justified Piedmontese annexation of the Romagna. The clericals in France were not more hysterical about this than were the English about the annexation of Savoy and Nice. To the former, their Charlemagne had become a Nebuchadnezzar; to the English the 'Alexander' of the nineteenth century had been revealed in his 'true' colours as a contemptible 'Annexander.'

Yet if the cession of Savoy and Nice was a crime, it was a crime in which from the beginning Cavour had been the Em-

peror's accomplice (as the English realized, though they tended to plead exten-
uating circumstances in Cavour's favour).
It had been part of the original bargain
to which Cavour had been a freely con-
senting party. If it was a violation of the
principle of Italy for the Italians, it was
a violation which Cavour had been willing to accept at Plombières, when he was
under no constraint whatever. Neither
Cavour nor Napoleon III had ever
assumed that Napoleon III was going to
help Italy for nothing. And to minimize
the service the Emperor rendered to Italy
is to ignore facts and fall victim to contemporary anti-Napoleonic hysteria in
England and the sedulously cultivated
prejudice against him that developed,
after Villafranca, in Italy. The work of
Cavour in the north and the centre up
to April 1860 depended as completely
on Napoleon III's initiative in attacking
the Habsburgs as Cavour's later work
depended on Garibaldi's initiative in attacking the Bourbons in the south. In
short, the contemptuous attitude usually
taken towards Napoleon III's work for
Italy is one of the shoddier bits of the
mythology of nineteenth century historians. Although he doubtless repented
of it after the cession of Nice, the fairer
verdict was Garibaldi's after Villafranca:
'Do not forget the gratitude we owe to
Napoleon III, and to the French army,
so many of whose valiant sons have been
killed or maimed for the cause of Italy.'

Thus the truth about Cavour is not
that he dared all for the national ideal,
never once stopping until the dream of
a united Italy had been fulfilled. Cavour
did not think national unity an aim that
justified the contemptuous violation of
all the normal rules of political and international conduct. His career does not,
as it has so often seemed to, provide a
precedent and an example of the notion
that an appeal to the principle of nationality makes war, double-dealing and
the fomentation of plots within the territories of other governments somehow
highly creditable actions which ought to
be applauded. Like Bismarck after him,
Cavour was both an anti-revolutionary
and an anti-nationalist. He saw clearly
that in practice the gospel of nationality
meant war without end. He was slower
than Napoleon III to see it, for Napoleon
realized it after Magenta and Solferino;
but in the end the outstanding work of
Cavour as an Italian statesman was not
to achieve Italian unification in 1860,
but to prevent it. That Rome and Venetia were not within the Kingdom of
Italy in 1861, in flat contradiction to the
declared aims of Garibaldi and the Radicals, but that what had been gained was
safe from all chance of foreign interference: these are the facts on which Cavour's claim to greatness rests. And facts
very like them are the basis of Bismarck's
greatness also.

A classic account of the *Risorgimento,* with Cavour
the unfaltering hero, was written in 1911 by Harvard
historian WILLIAM ROSCOE THAYER (1859–1923),
an ardent Protestant and liberal of the nineteenth-
century type. According to the 1961 *American
Historical Association Guide to Historical Literature,*
it is the "best biography of Cavour in any language."
In Thayer's judgment there can be no doubt that
whatever Giuseppe Mazzini's contributions to Italian
nationalism may have been in the quarter century
before 1849, they were a hindrance thereafter. Thayer's
harsh opinion may be balanced with that of Luigi
Salvatorelli in the next selection.*

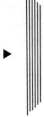

Mazzinianism: Hindrance to Unification

If Europe in the nineteenth century
bore any prophet of the celestial lineage,
Joseph Mazzini was he.

But immense injustice has been done
to Mazzini the Prophet by confounding
him with Mazzini the Politician. Nothing could be more preposterous than the
claim that, having been the forerunner,
he must therefore be the best pilot to
Italian Unity. If Piedmont had taken his
advice after 1850, there would have been
neither independence nor unity; if his
own Party of Action had followed him,
Italy would never have been freed or
united. Beginning with his tragical fiasco

at Milan in February, 1853, he proved
by the mad enterprises which he insti-
gated and by the wild propaganda which
he poured forth, that he misunderstood
the time, the men, the means. He not
only lost all sense of proportion, but deceived himself by supposing that his
formulas would work automatically, ir-
respective alike of the intelligence and
special aptitude of the Italians or of their
previous training. If he had had his way
there would have been no Crimean Expedition, no spokesman for Italy at the
Congress of Paris, no agreement at Plombières, no War of 1859 which resulted in

---

* From William Roscoe Thayer, *The Life and Times of Cavour* (Boston and New York: Houghton Mifflin Company, 1911), vol. II, pp. 431-432. Reprinted by permission of Houghton Mifflin
Company.

the liberation of Lombardy and the union of the Centre. Instead, there might have been civil war in Genoa and a succession of tragically inept conspiracies.

But far worse than his abortive opposition—which, after all, merely proved that he never

> Knew the seasons when to take
> Occasion by the hand—

was Mazzini's ten-year-long sowing of discord. Thanks to his genius for invective, seldom equaled and never surpassed, he planted in the hearts of many Italians distrust or hatred of the monarchical majority without which Unity could not have been achieved. He imputed selfish motives to the King, he vilified Cavour, he set circulating the poisonous insinuation that the Peninsula was to be Piedmontized, he scornfully reproved Manin and other Republicans who recognized that the time had come to unite under the King's leadership, and when the National Society drew nine-tenths of his party away from him, he reviled that. Then, the seeds of his sowing having borne fruit after their kind in factions and feuds, he protested that he was the champion of Unity, a peace-maker, a conciliator. That he believed this, who can question? Mazzini would always be reconciled to any opponent who submitted to him. But there is no appeal from Pallavicino's indictment: "Your presence divides us."

An incisive and indefatigable historian, LUIGI SALVATORELLI (1886–   ) has been equally at home in a university, newspaper office, or political party headquarters. From 1921 to 1925 he was joint managing editor of Turin's influential liberal daily, *La Stampa*. Dismissed by the Fascist dictatorship, he turned to historical research in a variety of fields and assumed an outspokenly republican position. In this passage, taken from his brilliant essays (first published in 1943) on the thought and action of the *Risorgimento*, Salvatorelli argues that the Mazzinians can take credit for pushing Cavour and Napoleon III into action in the 1850s.*

Unification Spurred by Mazzinianism

Orsini's assassination plot [against Napoleon III in 1858] provided the final inducement to [the Emperor to look after Italy's interests]. This is true no matter whether one prefers to emphasize the political and idealistic angle or to emphasize the worry that "Caesar" felt for his own personal safety. The fact is that out of it came the Plombières meeting, which provides the true point of departure for 1859—for the period in which the Italian political *Risorgimento* was achieved. It is not a case of direct continuity from the Crimean War and the Congress of Paris [1856] but rather of a new start—a start by Napoleon III, but undertaken because of the decisive influence of the Action Party and Mazzini. The fact that the latter took no part in the Orsini plot in no wise changes this conclusion—because in Napoleon III's view, the assassination plot formed a part, and rightly so, of the whole pattern of Mazzinian activity.

Mazzini and Cavour

One should not infer from this that there was a perfect complementary relationship (real even though impersonal)

* From Luigi Salvatorelli, *Pensiero e azione del Risorgimento*, 6th edition (Turin: Giulio Einaudi Editore, 1960), pp. 151-157, 163-165, translated by Charles F. Delzell. Reprinted by permission of Giulio Einaudi Editore.

between the Cavour of this final phase and Mazzini—unless one wishes to revert to the school of historical interpretation that would reduce the *Risorgimento* to a process of steady territorial expansion on the part of the House of Savoy. Indeed, for such an interpretation, it would be quite easy to conjoin the work of Mazzini and Cavour, and to link historically these two men who as flesh-and-blood individuals hated each other so cordially. (Actually, however, the adherents to this historical theory prefer to eliminate Mazzini as much as possible.) No one would deny that Mazzini was the oldest and most tenacious propagandist of Italian unification and the unitary Italian state. Nor can or does anyone contest the primary efficacy of his work in this regard. No one, moreover, can doubt that a unitary Italian state arose between 1859 and 1861 around the nucleus of the Piedmontese state (Venetia and Rome were fated completions to an edifice already in existence), or that this work of aggregation was completed under the political and governing direction of Count Cavour.

If the question is posed in this fashion, everything boils down to a discussion of how and when. Which of the two did the more? The less? When did Cavour first take up the cause of Italian unity? What part did he play in the expedition of the Thousand? Who was responsible for the idea and the initiative for the expedition into the Marches and Umbria? How did Rome come to be proclaimed capital of Italy? Undoubtedly these specific questions are of great interest, but their diverse solutions do not radically change the overall picture. If one considers the *Risorgimento* to have been fully achieved by 1870 according to the only method

possible, then all the programs and forces that had a part in it appear, purely and simply, absorbed and transcended [*superati*].

If, however, one goes beyond the simple consideration of the political and territorial expansion, one observes that the Italian unitary, monarchical, constitutional, and parliamentary state which was formed between 1860 and 1870 displayed several characteristics that were contrary to the Mazzinian ideals and program. It would be incorrect to say that Mazzini and Cavour worked together (unless one makes clear the role of each) for a result which, combining their work, entirely transcended them and absorbed them both. In reality, a victor and a vanquished emerged from the struggle. The victor was Cavour, the vanquished Mazzini. Or to be more precise, Mazzini won in the first round, imposing the unitary program on Piedmontese "municipalism," but in the carrying out of this program, Mazzini succumbed. And even more than he . . . radical liberalism —self-government of a federal, republican type—succumbed.

In the process of achieving Italian unity the real question was how, by whom, and for whom this unity would be accomplished. The question of monarchy versus republic involved a deeper conflict between Cavour and Mazzini. Mazzini's fixed idea was that of an Italian popular uprising. If this meant, with respect to foreign powers, that Italy must do the job herself and ahead of other peoples, it meant, with respect to domestic considerations, that the Italian people must themselves rise up and achieve unification, for "revolutions have to be made for the people and by the people." Hence, in an open letter from Florence on Sepember 20, 1859, Mazzini rebuked King Victor Emmanuel II: "You did not act like a brother of the People of Italy, nor did you call them to join you as a brother. educed by the sad policy of a ministry hat preferred the art of Lodovico il Moro to that of a regenerator, you rejected the arm of our People and in an nauspicious hour needlessly called for military help from a foreign tyrant, asking him to serve as an ally in a liberating enterprise."

Here, too, one cannot reduce the dispute between Mazzini and Cavour to a simple difference in evaluating practical possibilities whereby the former believed that Italy could "go it alone" against Austria (as King Charles Albert had insisted) and the latter did not. Nor can it be reduced simply to Mazzinian doctrinairism and refusal of the help of a tyrant," in contrast to Cavourian opportunism. Beyond all this, Mazzini sensed intuitively, with the clairvoyance of his passionate nature, that the French alliance was something more than a practical expedient, that it was the means for transforming the Italian national and popular cause into a monarchist and governmental undertaking. On June 9, 1860, during Senate discussion of the treaty that ceded Nice and Savoy, Cavour remarked, "Senator Pallavicino loves the alliance with revolution first of all and that with France only secondarily." Cavour did not intend these words as a token of praise for Pallavicino. Indeed, for Cavour the order of preference was the opposite: revolutions, even when they are national, should be employed as little as possible. More than once, in fact, he set forth "national" against "revolutionary," meaning by the former adjective the national, monarchical movement

in favor of the House of Savoy. It is well known that Cavour even went so far as audaciously to plan, as a firm decision, that Piedmont would renew the war with Austria on its own if Garibaldi and the Action Party triumphed in the Kingdom of Naples; and that he did so to restore to the monarchy the initiative that it had lost in the national movement. "For a prince of the House of Savoy, it is better to perish in a war than in a revolution."

Between Mazzini and Cavour, therefore, it was a struggle between two kinds of initiatives: a popular and revolutionary one (intended by Mazzini to remain as such even when he accepted the monarchy) as against a monarchical and governmental one. Here they were irreconcilable. In the interval between the Villafranca armistice and the plebiscite in Naples, Mazzini's program was to stay neutral between republic and monarchy, to make sure that the final decision should be deferred to a vote by a national constituent assembly. As to the outcome of the vote he had no doubts, but he contended that having a monarchy created *ex novo* by popular vote would be quite a different thing from merely adding the various parts of Italy to an already existing monarchy.

Cavour and Victor Emmanuel also recognized this, but they formulated an opposite pattern of practical conduct. There is no reason to think that Cavour was not entirely firm in his monarchical and dynastic feeling just because he had detested Charles Albert and been replaced by him, or because he never reached full understanding with Victor Emmanuel. Cavour's constant antirepublicanism (save for a brief period—only a moment—in his early youth) was an integral part of his hostility to revolutions and his aversion to popular governments and popular initiatives, and it coincided with his fear of communism.

However, this antirevolutionism of Cavour, this determined aversion to popular uprisings, this overriding concern to keep leadership of the national movement in the hands of the royal government, did not reflect interests on his part that were solely dynastic and conservative. In all of this there was also a liberal moment. In September 1860, at the time of sharp conflict with Garibaldi, he said it was not merely a matter of personalities, but that two systems were in conflict, for Garibaldi dreamed of a kind of dictatorship with no parliament and little freedom. (As a matter of fact, Garibaldi's tendency to favor a "national dictatorship" . . . was utilized by Victor Emmanuel and by Cavour to the advantage of the monarchy.) A little later, in his famous letter of December 29, 1860, to Countess de Circourt, Cavour set forth, in antithesis, freedom versus a dictatorship of popular origin. And rejecting the advice of General Filangieri to make himself dictator, he eloquently proclaimed in an almost lyrical outburst his faith in parliamentary liberalism.

In contrast to Cavour's faith in parliament, Mazzini remained firm in his aversion to constitutional monarchy. His first thought in this respect dated back to 1834: "Constitutional monarchy is the most immoral government in the world—an essentially corrupting institution; because the organized struggle that forms the vitality of such a government stirs up all the individual passions to the conquest of honors or of the fortune that alone gives access to honors."

Here we touch on a basic conflict in ideas—let us even say a conflict between the two men's views of the world. Cavour did not shy away in the least from "organized struggle" (even though occasionally, as in the persecution of *Italia del Popolo,* it happened that in practice he changed the rules of the game). And unlike the moralist Mazzini, he was not at all inclined to be shocked by the "stirring up" of individual passions. Once he said in Parliament that he could not imagine a system based on freedom that did not include parties or struggles. Complete, absolute peace was incompatible with freedom, which one must be willing to accept with its benefits and "perhaps also its inconveniences." Mazzini, too, intended to preserve freedom, but he envisaged a state of affairs in which partisan struggle would come naturally to an end: "Duty, once admitted, excludes the possibility of struggle." This was the Mazzinian ideal of unity, the "dogma" of unity, as he himself said, which for him (we know) went well beyond political unity. The latter was only a prerequisite for moral and religious unity.

Thus there is a dual aspect to the dispute between Mazzini and Cavour. Insofar as the former advocated popular uprisings in contrast to the latter (who was a jealous guardian of the principle of action by the monarchical government), it was Mazzini who was the more liberal the more radical innovator. But with respect to the ideal of uniformity that Mazzini conceived as the culmination of his philosophy, in contrast to Cavour's belief in ceaseless political struggle, one must reach an opposite judgment. This second contrast derived from the particular mental make-up of the two men. Cavour rationalistically distinguished between politics and religion (or moral ity), whereas Mazzini mystically fused them. No doubt laic rationalism and religious mysticism were quite opposite characteristics of Cavour and Mazzini, yet this does not mean that Cavour was indifferent to religious problems. Indeed, it was in this field . . . that he attained his highest idealism. Nor does this antithesis in mentality and spiritual aspirations of the two men necessarily signify an intrinsic or irreducible opposition between their separate goals, which actually represented exigencies that were equally profound and equally necessary for the unfolding of the historical process. From this standpoint, one can again speak (on a much higher plane than that of immediate political accomplishments) of the complementary relationship of Mazzini and Cavour.

Italian unification was achieved between April 1859 and March 1861—one might even say between April 1859 and October 1860—in other words, within a tremendously brief span of time. Territorially, there had been no unity since the time of the Lombard invasion thirteen centuries earlier, and unitary self-government had never existed. This consideration alone is enough to show the absurdity of the thesis (if it is not honoring it too much to use this term) that would reduce the *Risorgimento* to a process of steady territorial expansion on the part of the House of Savoy. The latter, after having taken seven hundred years to push out of the Alps as far as the Ticino River, would, according to this interpretation, all by itself, by its miraculous intrinsic strength, swallow up in two years all the rest of Italy! Such an enormous disparity can be explained only if one understands that quite different and deeper forces played a part in unification—a century-long, moral and political process, which by a concatenation of circumstances achieved in the course of two years the territorial political result that was an essential aspect, but neither the only nor the supreme aspect, of the *Risorgimento*. Indeed, the prodigious speed of the achievement offers one more reason to investigate whether some constitutional imperfection was not hidden by it.

These were the extraordinarily concurrent circumstances: a popular initiative (namely, revolutions in central Italy, the expedition of the Thousand, and projects and efforts to tear down all temporal power); a political and military action by the House of Savoy; and multiple aspects of the European situation—that is, in addition to the Franco-Piedmontese alliance and to Napoleon III's policy, the policy of Palmerston and Russell that was favorable to Italian unity, the Austrian internal crisis, the rivalry between Austria and Prussia, and, even more important, the disagreement between Austria and Russia.

During the prophetic biennium, the monarchy (and Cavour in behalf of it) acted as the mediating factor (in its own self-interest quite apart from that of Italy) between the popular initiative and European politics. The mediation was the work of extraordinary political ability, and in view of the complexity of factors to be conciliated was superior to even the finest diplomatic achievements of Bismarck. But mediation could not have taken place if there had been no terms to mediate. It was at this point that the popular initiative came from Mazzini, or at least the initiative was Mazzinian in its direct or indirect source and inspiration (as, for example, the work of the Italian National Society). Another influence alongside this was radical liberalism. Thus it would be quite unhistorical to regard (out of respect for the demiurge or *deus ex machina* [1] of Victor Emmanuel II or Cavour) Mazzini's actions after 1849—and particularly during the decisive two years—as being ineffective or downright damaging, or as being an obstacle to the work that was accomplished.

The Franco-Piedmontese war against Austria in 1859 was not the event most important in bringing about Italian unification; by itself the war could have produced no more than a Kingdom of Upper Italy and a confederation—in other words, a return to the [program of the 1848 era]—and according to Napoleon III's formal intentions, it was not intended to accomplish more than this. The three most important events in bringing about unity were: the insurrections in central Italy, the expedition to Sicily, and the expedition into the Marches and Umbria. All three were Mazzinian-inspired examples of "thought and action," and popular and revolutionary enterprises. The first two were achieved, at least in their initial impetus, as popular revolutions. (It will be recalled that the Tuscan revolution of April 27 [1859], the most important among those in central Italy, was chiefly the work of the Action Party.) The expedition of the Thousand, with Garibaldi as its popular hero *par excellence,* was, furthermore, the epitome of insurrection and guerrilla-type warfare. The third event was accomplished by the monarchy, which adopted [Mazzini's type of approach] as its own idea, by actually initiating a popular revolution. And the monarchy made it its own—as one can see from Cavour's letters of the time—because it held that this was the only way to save itself and prevent Italian unification from proceeding in a republican direction. Once more, and just at the right moment, came into play the dilemma that Victor Emmanuel II had seen clearly—of becoming either King of Italy or just "Monsú Savoia" [Mr. Savoy].

Mazzini gave in and accepted the leading role of the monarchy and actually promoted it, even though he foresaw that the result would be contrary to his own republican ideal. He did this because the desire for unity—in this case territorial rather than political and moral unity—predominated over everything else. He certainly reserved to himself and to his followers the right of political opposition —of continuing propaganda in behalf of republican ideals. Thus even he—who was considered by so many people to be a stubborn sectarian, the oppositionist pure and simple, the idealist with head in the clouds—perceived the political reality and was able to adapt himself to it in the supreme interest of the nation. Actually, from his point of view, the question to be faced was whether he had not adapted himself too much. It was a magnanimous sacrifice, an extreme example of *sic vos non vobis.*[2] Was this not the reason there was persistent hostility between him and the new order of things —hostility that transformed the chief apostle of the unitary state, as soon as unity was achieved, into the conspirator and nonconformist that he remained until his death?

[1] Something artificially introduced to solve a problem.—*Ed.*

[2] Acting not in one's own best interests.—*Ed.*

Like Salvatorelli, ADOLFO OMODEO (1889–1946) was one of the first in Italy to discuss the *Risorgimento* in terms of the broader context of European history. Unfortunately Omodeo's political biography of Cavour was left uncompleted at his death. In this excerpt from it Omodeo argues that Mazzini was certainly no nonentity in 1859 and that his hostility to Cavour was cleverly utilized by the latter to resist Napoleonic domination of Italy.

Again like Salvatorelli, Omodeo entered politics after the overthrow of Mussolini in 1943 and helped found a new Action Party that was uncompromisingly republican in its hostility to the House of Savoy, which had come to be tarnished by Fascism.*

Mazzinianism: Leverage for Cavour against Napoleon

[In 1859] the prophet [Mazzini] experienced the infinite bitterness of seeing his work collapse and himself abandoned. Gritting his teeth at the shame of seeing Italy emerge thanks to French intervention, he declared that he had little esteem for those Italians who had not responded to his ardent appeals to re-establish a fatherland and who, out of regard for a foreign despot, seemed to forget liberty and unity. Yet he did not slow down his work. He spread the alarm through Europe that Louis [Napoleon] Bonaparte wanted to attempt a European *coup d'état;* he desperately sought to excite the people toward unity; he paralyzed the Bonapartist maneuvers in central Italy for a separate kingdom under Prince Jerome Napoleon; he sought to broaden the Italian movement by encouraging Garibaldi in 1859 to move beyond Cattolica [southward into the Papal States]. He sailed against the current and felt himself failing in strength; yet he still deluded himself into thinking that he might win.

For him too the acme of this terrible contest occurred in the spring of 1859, when he had to take a stand against the Franco-Sardinian War [with Austria]. He

* From Adolfo Omodeo, *L'opera politica del conte di Cavour*, parte I (1848-1857), vol. II, 2nd edition (Florence: La Nuova Italia Editrice, 1941), pp. 229-232, translated by Charles F. Delzell. Reprinted by permission of La Nuova Italia Editrice.

resembled that ancient popular tribune who, while hurling maledictions, had accompanied the army of Crassus that was marching against the Parthians. His secessionist friends warned him not to interfere with the Piedmontese effort and intimated to him that they would use the party funds to back up the war. Alberto Mario vacillated in his republicanism, and even the faithful Jessie could not hide from him her admiration for Garibaldi. His remaining followers were uncertain and hesitant. This was the abandoned prophet's hour of Gethsemane.

Yet even in that isolation and moral detachment from a nation at war, his task had not come to an end. Despite all superficial judgments, it was of capital importance for Italy.

For Mazzini was a political reserve force that would go into action against any excessive French demand. Italy was no longer the Italy of the era of Charles VIII [of France], and Napoleon had to keep this in mind. Mazzini, with his record, with his legend, might suddenly rise up again, just as he had in 1848 after the failure of the royalists' war. (As late as May 1860 Baron Talleyrand, the French representative at Turin, feared such a Mazzinian nightmare.)

From London [Mazzini] anxiously followed Cavour's policy, which was on the verge of shipwreck—and Mazzini desired that it go down—on the shoals of the international congress that was being demanded by hostile diplomats. If it did, the situation would be reversed. The immense disillusionment that would ensue could again bring back to his side all the Italians who had uselessly been cajoled and excited into war by the Franco-Piedmontese diplomatic conspiracy. The revolutionary explosion would follow

thereafter, in accordance with the methods and predictions of Mazzini. It would be up to the exile to confiscate for himself the preparatory work done by Cavour. Mazzini, the abandoned prophet, would have regained incalculable power if only one small thing had occurred—for example, if Cavour had actually fired a bullet into his brain on the night of April 18–19, 1859, after receipt of the diplomatic warning; or if Austria had delayed her ultimatum only a few days.

Certainly events were working against him, and politically he was beaten and in error. But such a strictly political judgment is too narrow. Both Mazzini and Cavour worked for Italy above and beyond any personal desire for success. The crux of the problem is this: unification of Italy required that somebody during the crisis of 1859 assume the unpopular stance that Mazzini had to take. It was not without importance that two possible courses of action remained open to Italy until the very end—either the moderate one of Cavour or the revolutionary one of the exile—and that there should be in existence a vigilant and multiple force which, as soon as the Austrians were expelled, could prevent the French from imposing firm hegemony in Italy. Mazzini feared that Napoleon's intervention in the peninsula might ruin the national cause for twenty or fifty years unless another force were interposed. It was Mazzini himself who furnished this force, even though it was in his role as a defeated party. The threat of Mazzinianism served to precipitate both the Emperor Napoleon and the Aulic Council of Vienna into war; and, at the same time, the exile without a following served to limit and check the French plan of action in Italy. In fact, he prevented the French from going beyond the bounds of strictly military assistance (whereas in 1848, when such military assistance had been requested of France, it had seemed to Bastide and to Cavaignac beneath the dignity of a great power like France). He created for Cavour a position of incomparable prestige in the face of his powerful ally. By means of his idealistic faith, Mazzini broadened the field of possible action for the Count [Cavour] beyond his own hopes.

One misfortune alone could cause Cavour to lose, and along with Cavour, Italy. This was that the hated and weakened antagonist [Mazzini] should lay down his arms and pass over into the Piedmontese camp. That would have deprived the Count of his fortress point of defense against French hegemony; he would have become a mere subaltern of Napoleon, who could then decide the fate of the peninsula whenever he saw fit. Once again, without intending to do so, Mazzini strengthened his rival.

Now this curious sequence of events whereby from time to time Mazzini and Cavour and Garibaldi each saw their own work corrected, restricted, and modified by reciprocal interaction; whereby each carried out a specific and distinct function, and their work fused together beyond their own intentions; and whereby they were frustrated in their own demiurgical ambitions and reduced to becoming mere parts of a much greater whole —all this is the mark of the vital reality of the Italian people, of that vital reality which numerous historians, allowing themselves to be misguided by a mythical fantasy on the part of Mazzini, have searched for but not found in the *masses.*

In this vision of the organic life of the Italian people, the historian can render justice to the vanquished. Certainly Mazzini was despoiled of the fruits of his work, and the limitations imposed by what is possible caused the results that were attained to be something less than his own universal and eschatological ideal. Nevertheless, the concrete formation of the Italian people gravitated for a moment about the adamantine faith of a Mazzini who would not give in. In that supreme moment the heart of Italy beat in unison with the heart of the sorrowing exile.

The question of Premier Cavour's real attitude toward the Sicilian expedition of Garibaldi and the Thousand in May 1860 is one of the most hotly debated subjects in *Risorgimento* history. In this excerpt from **WILLIAM ROSCOE THAYER**'s invaluable *Life and Times of Cavour,* the author vigorously defends Cavour's attitude toward Garibaldi at the time of the invasion. He has no doubts but that Cavour's government connived to help Garibaldi, and actually furnished him aid.*

Garibaldi's Sicilian Expedition Facilitated by Cavour

Cavour's attitude towards the projected Sicilian Expedition has been the most criticized by his enemies of all his political acts. Not even the cession of Nice supplied them with so unfailing a secretion of venom. And yet, although all the documents have not been published, and much oral testimony is lost forever, we can almost unerringly trace his course, surmise the reason for each decision and for each change of front, and if we do this dispassionately we cannot escape the conclusion that he was guided throughout by the keenest foresight and by the highest patriotism. The funda-

mental mistake made by Mazzini, and by later critics who have echoed his vituperation, is that they identified their own program with Italy itself. When, therefore, Cavour differed from them, he was indisputably, according to their argument, a traitor to Italy. . . .

. . . The Sicilian Expedition, which the world saluted as the noblest offspring of modern chivalry, . . . was no sudden creation.[1] Had it depended on Garibaldi

[1] This episode, the most thorny in the history of the Risorgimento, is discussed by the biographers of all the leading participants, by historians, and by essayists. Recent reviews of the evidence have been made by A. Luzio, *Corriere*

* From William Roscoe Thayer, *The Life and Times of Cavour* (Boston and New York: Houghton Mifflin Company, 1911), vol. II, pp. 237, 267-269, omitting most of the original footnotes. Reprinted by permission of Houghton Mifflin Company.

alone, the expedition would never have started; without Garibaldi, it could never have started. La Masa, Medici, Bixio, could not have drawn after them the host triumphant, nor the universal popular sympathy which even Diplomacy dared not ignore. Mazzini planned; Crispi prepared; Bertani organized; Bixio at the critical moment acted. Of the many other aiders in the preparations, Rosalino Pilo and Corrao, the Precursors who sped unsupported into Sicily, deserve unstinted praise: but for them, the preliminary revolt might have died out.

Equally necessary was the connivance of the Government. Garibaldi has denounced Cavour for not openly equipping the Expedition: but this is an unfair charge, for it was Garibaldi himself who up to the last moment believed the adventure doomed to fail and refused to embark on it. If Garibaldi distrusted Mazzini, had not Cavour greater reason to distrust him? If Garibaldi, who had only his own reputation at stake, hesitated until he was assured that success was almost certain, how much more was it the duty of Cavour to hold back an exploit which, if fortunate, might bring down on free Italy the wrath of Europe, and, if Garibaldi perished, would arouse against the Monarchy the frenzy of millions of Italians! Actions speak louder than words. The freedom with which the conspirators were allowed to make their arrangements; the constant communications between their leaders and the Cavourians: their interviews with Cavour himself, with the King, with Farini; the public subscriptions voted by Cremona, Pavia, Brescia, and other cities, without hint of interference from Turin; the gathering of the volunteers unmolested at Genoa, not once but twice; the studied

inattention of the Genoese officials to the final preparations; the gift to Garibaldi of the National Society's guns and ammunitions, without which he would not have sailed; the failure to order Persano to intercept the ships—these are facts which, singly and collectively, give the lie to the slander that Cavour and the King's Government refused to aid the enterprise. That slander sprang partly from envy, because Garibaldians and Mazzinians wished to take entire credit to themselves, and especially to have it appear that the Monarchists whom they hated could not share in any patriotic undertaking; and partly it sprang from Garibaldi's unreasoning hatred of Cavour. When that hatred was planted in his soul, and constantly nurtured by the evil suggestions of designing associates, Garibaldi interpreted by it every act of Cavour. Quite incapable of grasping the intricacy of Piedmont's international relations, on which her very existence depended, he accused Cavour of treachery and servility for heeding those relations; believing in a dictatorship with himself at its head as the panacea for social and political ills, he hated Cavour, who, as a constitutional minister, could not countenance would-be dictators. Garibaldi's hatred made him oblivious of speaking the truth. In a single page of his "Memoirs" he accuses Cavour of having abandoned a few months before, against the King's orders, the Hunters of the Alps to the Austrians—a baseless falsehood. He accuses Cavour of sequestrating the fifteen

della Sera, May 5 and Aug. 23, 1907; by I. Raulich, *Rass. Contempo.*, July, 1909; and by R. Mirabelli, *Secolo*, Sept. 16, 17, 18, 1907, and *Rivista Popolare*, Jan. 15 and 31, 1910; by H. N. Gay, *Deutsche Revue,* Dec. 1910. For extreme Radical position see N. Colajanni's articles in *Rivista Popolare*, 1910.

thousand muskets at Milan—a baseless falsehood, as D'Azeglio's letter to Rendu, published in 1867, and his letter to Persano, published in 1869, prove. He accuses Cavour of getting a factitious popularity by buying up men and newspapers with the nation's money—a falsehood not only baseless but puerile. How should we judge Garibaldi, if we accepted as infallible Tennyson's maxim: "Every one imputes himself"? The test of zeal is not its intensity but its purpose: zeal forges alike the Anarchist and the Jesuit. Chivalry is picturesque, romantic exploits thrill: but no hero should feel himself absolved from obligation to speak the truth; and mankind has been better served in the long run by lovers of justice than by zealots.

It was well for Italy that Garibaldi's venomous charges against Cavour were not true. If none but approved Garibaldians had gone on the Expedition though they had conquered Sicily and Naples, they would have postponed, perhaps for decades, the day of National Unity. Only by the participation, however indirect and unofficial, of the Monarchy in the preparations could the indispensable all-Italian quality be secured. This was Cavour's work. When he was convinced, says Guerzoni, "that the cry for Sicily was not the artifice of one man alone or of one party, but the clear deep echo of a sentiment of the whole nation, then he hesitated no longer, but conceded to the preparers all that the ruler of a constitutional State had a right to concede: power to make ready, to arm, and to set sail under the shadow of his Government and under the shield of his King."

Formerly of Cambridge University and now at All Souls' College, Oxford, DENIS MACK SMITH (1920–   ) is one of the most penetrating and controversial writers on modern Italian history. Like his mentor, George Macaulay Trevelyan, he is enchanted by the flamboyant Garibaldi. The first part of this selection comes from a paper Mack Smith read to the Cambridge Historical Society on December 2, 1948.* In contrast to Thayer's interpretation of the facts in the previous selection, his verdict is that Cavour was less than helpful to Garibaldi's expedition to Sicily. The concluding paragraphs come from Mack Smith's monograph, *Cavour and Garibaldi, 1860: A Study in Political Conflict*,† in which he argues that Cavour was "sometimes treacherous, often uncertain, . . . always more or less hostile to Garibaldi," and *"necessarily* all of these things."

Cavour Hostile and Treacherous to Garibaldi

There is always likely to be disagreement over the question of how great a part is played in historical events by deliberate human decision. Fundamentally, this may not be a question for the historian as an historian; yet it is bound to concern him, and all the more so as he turns from economic history or the rise and fall of civilizations, and instead brings his microscope to bear on the day-to-day problems of diplomacy or administration. Sometimes it is thought that this narrowing of the focus from the centuries down to the weeks and days will by itself bring a readjustment of view in favour of free will and the effectiveness of human decisions. But, in fact, it may as easily have the contrary result; and if a succession of events is looked at in sufficient detail, it may happen that conscious human agency again recedes into the shadow. A statesman may then appear to be moved less by previously formulated policy than by a march of small events which collectively seem to carry him on—sometimes so much so that only

* From Denis Mack Smith, "Cavour's Attitude to Garibaldi's Expedition to Sicily," *The Cambridge Historical Journal,* vol. IX (1949), pp. 359–370, omitting many of the original footnotes. Reprinted by permission of both the author and the Kraus Reprint Corporation, New York.

† From Denis Mack Smith, *Cavour and Garibaldi, 1860: A Study in Political Conflict* (Cambridge, England: University Press, 1954), pp. 436–443, omitting the original footnotes. Reprinted by permission of Cambridge University Press.

in courtesy can we say that he had any policy at all. A good statesman has been defined as one who does not coerce events but cooperates with them. Yet as we watch the relations between a sequence of happenings and the working of a man's mind, it frequently appears as if such co-operation is just the coercion exercised on men by events, and that statesmanship is really to be found in qualities of passivity and resilience which accept this hard fact and make what they can of it.

Cavour was one of the first great statesmen to live in the telegraph age when the minute-to-minute study of history becomes possible. He is justly renowned for his remarkable *tact des choses possibles* [feeling for what is feasible], and it was he who said that 'history is a great improviser.' Yet when he came to look back, he himself like the rest of us rationalized his career, idealized his motives, and superimposed a pattern on the past. His biographers have gone even further, since historians as well as scientists are most happy when they can render down a hopelessly complicated tangle of facts into a simple pattern. There is, however, no necessary reason why truth should be beautiful or simple; and if we examine Cavour's attitude at the moment when Garibaldi set out with his piratical venture on 5 May 1860, we shall find it almost impossible to summarize his activity in any formula or pattern that is consistent with all the facts.

In so far as there may be said to be any orthodox opinion among historians, it is held that Cavour gave to Garibaldi every help consistent with diplomatic prudence. On this view Cavour was by now at last convinced of the possibility of unifying Italy, and was already himself

forming plans for invading the south.[1] When the evidence seems to show both persecution of, and assistance to, Garibaldi, this is generally explained as real but secret assistance merely disguised by pretended persecution. The most balanced and moderate supporters of this view, like the Master of Trinity, do add that it is still impossible to make all the facts fit such a pattern, and confess that they cannot fully fathom his motives—indeed, that Cavour probably changed his mind more than once.[2]

Alternatively, it might be held that on this matter Cavour scarcely had any mind to change, and that like most politicians most of the time he rather drifted before events. His motives on this view would seem a little more ascertainable, though still complicated enough; it was partly because of their complexity that he was unable to face the problem with a fully consistent policy which would have enabled us to reduce his actions to a coherent pattern. But it is always a weakness of the empirical statesmen who co-operate with events that when history does surprise them with an unexpected alternative they are often not ready to make up their minds in time to influ-

[1] La Farina: 'Cavour's party helped the expedition with every possible means,' *Atti Parlamentari*, 18 June 1863. I. Nazari-Micheli: 'Certainly this help had to be given covertly, and even be concealed behind a pretended persecution. . . . But no-one can deny any longer that Cavour helped the Sicilian insurrection from March 24 onwards, and the expedition of the Thousand from the time of its preparation,' *Cavour e Garibaldi nel 1860* (1911), pp. 194–5. See also N. Bianchi, *Il Conte Camillo di Cavour* (1863), p. 91; P. Matter, *Cavour et l'Unité Italienne* (1927), iii, 342; D. Zanichelli, *Cavour* (1926), p. 376.

[2] G. M. Trevelyan, *Garibaldi and the Thousand* (1909), p. 198. This is still, after forty years, the best and most readable account of the events of 1860.

ence those events. In this case the facts are best explained if it is assumed that there was a hiatus in Cavour's policy, just at the most critical moment in the whole *risorgimento,* when Italy came near to foreign invasion and civil war, when Cavour's government on his own confession was tottering, and when the revolutionary party was ready to supplant him with its republican or federalist solutions to the Italian problem.[3] Not only this, but it may be further argued that such influence as Cavour did have on events in these few days was used less to help than to deter and thwart Garibaldi.

It is true that this interpretation contradicts the opinion generally prevailing in the hagiolatry which passes most often in Italy for *risorgimento* history. It was a view once propounded by the radical politicians in opposition to Cavour, and then discredited along with their politics. Because nineteenth-century Italian history is still part of present-day party politics, it is often interpreted for this reason with passion and even becomes falsified. It has, for instance, been assumed in official historiography that Cavour *must* have been right, and hence must be proved right. Also there was the myth forged by the fascists to prove that they derived equally from the three heroes of the *risorgimento,* from the prophet Mazzini, the statesman Cavour, and the soldier Garibaldi; for which reason the official historians of the *régime* had to prove that these three men had been working harmoniously together for the greatness of Italy. The importance Mussolini attributed to this sort of work is shown by the fact that he appointed as Director-General of Historical Research no less a man than Maria De Vecchi di

Val Cismon, one of the notorious quadrumvirate who commanded his march on Rome. But this subordination of history to politics under fascism was nothing new, for the old liberal historians had preceded the Italian nationalists in taking over the heroics of their recent past and appropriating them to a political creed. Before Mussolini was born the greater part of Cavour's correspondence had been successively edited by state-paid archivists who (admirable though their work was in many respects) chose to rewrite passages in the letters before publication, and were always scrupulous to save his reputation from any imprudent revelations that might damage the traditional portrait. A Royal Commission was formed in 1910 ostensibly to remedy this with a more trustworthy text, but even now after forty years it has still not published the volumes concerned with Cavour's attitude to Garibaldi's expedition; and in the meantime either the narrow vanity of archivists or reasons of state have kept the documents under lock and key, closed even to the most distinguished of Italian scholars.[4]

Perhaps now with the end of fascism has also ended what might be called the heroic phase of *risorgimento* history writing. The legends are being a little deflated now that the making of Italy is seen to be not altogether the liberal, liberating movement it once seemed, and its heroes to be less heroic and perhaps less important. Historical revision is

---

[3] This suggestion of a hiatus was maintained by A. Omodeo, *Tradizioni Morali e Disciplina Storica* (1929), p. 215.

[4] The first volume of Cavour's correspondence on *La liberazione del mezzogiorno* has just appeared (Aug. 1949), but too late for use in the preparation of this article. It is edited by the new Royal Commission under Bonomi, and published by Zanichelli.

showing, for example, that the growing prosperity of Piedmont was not solely due to Cavour, but went back to the time of Charles Albert; or again, that Cavour's foreign policy was not materially different from the traditional policy of the House of Savoy; or thirdly, that among Cavour's objectives there did not figure the unification of Italy if the price to be paid for it included either upsetting the monarchy or ending the dominant position of Piedmont in the peninsula. Far from working harmoniously with the republican Mazzini, Cavour was in May 1860 harrying him with secret agents, determined on his arrest as a criminal under double sentence of death. The Sicilian expedition was known to be Mazzini's favourite scheme; and though Garibaldi was not himself so dogmatic in his republicanism, he was surrounded at Genoa by republican hotheads who would reap any benefit there was likely to be gained from the affair, and whose manifest intention it was to win over the Neapolitan army and fleet and use them to take over from Cavour the leadership in the Italian revolution.[5] For such reasons Cavour naturally opposed the expedition. Not a round of ammunition did he give to the Thousand; not a penny either, though pennies could have been easily and secretly given, and would have been most welcome.

But almost at once a legend grew up to the contrary, based on the two indisputable facts, first that Cavour did not positively stop Garibaldi's departure, and secondly, that he did actively help the next expedition which followed thirty-five days later, once half Sicily had been conquered. One can watch this legend appearing in the French Yellow Book on Garibaldi's expedition, which omitted a phrase in the original report of their

ambassador calling it an unqualified Mazzinian plot; for by the time the Yellow Book was published the French attitude, like that of Cavour himself, had changed to recognition of Garibaldi's staggering and unforeseen success, and the desire both to make it respectable and to profit from it. Garibaldi himself unwittingly added to the legend, because he found local authorities more co-operative if he wore a Piedmontese general's uniform to which he was not entitled, and if he assured them that he was acting in connivance with the government. The conservative ministers of Europe contributed still more to the legend, for they naturally tried their hardest to make out that Cavour was responsible. But Cavour himself was its most effective propagator. His elaborate smoke screen was used to delude not only France and Naples but also every shade of Italian politician into thinking he was really on their side, for he wished to keep open every avenue of escape until events had chosen for him the policy he was unwilling to choose himself.[6] Whichever interpretation of his actions is adopted, Ca-

[5] Two letters to Cavour from Farini, the Minister of the Interior, dated 24 and 25 Apr. 1860: 'the king told these gentlemen of the Left straight out that his own Ministers meant to keep a tight hold of policy and not let the initiative be taken out of their hands by Garibaldi or anyone'; 'a crisis at the moment would naturally bring the radicals into power.' *Carte Farini*, in the Biblioteca Classense at Ravenna.

[6] In a despatch of 30 Mar., the French Minister Talleyrand told Thouvenel that Cavour, when asked what he would do if Sicily revolted against Naples, had replied: 'Si l'insurrection est comprimée nous ne dirons rien: si elle est victorieuse nous interviendrons au nom des principes d'ordre et d'autorité.' ['If the insurrection is compromised, we shall say nothing about it; if it is victorious, we shall intervene in the name of the principles of order and authority.'] (This is precisely what he did do.) C. Maraldi, *Documenti francesi sulla caduta del regno meridionale* (1935), pp. 30–1. . . .

vour must have been lying to half the people he spoke to. Among those who knew him well neither Lord John Russell, nor Cavour's predecessor as Prime Minister, D'Azeglio, could easily believe again that he meant what he said.[7] It was surely the nemesis of Machiavellianism when on the one hand people ceased to believe him and on the other hand he deceived even his own supporters. And the historian who now looks at a letter of Cavour must ask every time, first whether there could be any possible reason for the author deceiving this particular correspondent; and secondly, if so, whether lies were not being used less to conceal a policy, than to disguise the absence of any policy. Thus the smoke screen blew back into Cavour's face, as well as obscuring the vision of historians ever since.

The fact was that his motives at this time cancelled one another out. To be on safe ground we can say little more than that he did have perfectly good reasons for not wanting the expedition to sail. Apart from its quasi-republican origin, there was the danger that it might involve him in war with Naples and Austria at a time when he was more anxious to consolidate his newly won provinces in northern Italy: it would also embroil him with France and invite Louis Napoleon's intervention just when he was trying to inveigle the French garrison of Rome back to France. Cavour's plans for Italy certainly included another war in the near future, possibly the following year, when it was to be hoped the French might march on Antwerp; but he naturally wanted to choose his own time for creating a revolutionary situation in Italy. If now Garibaldi became Duce of a revolutionary army and Dictator of the two Sicilies, such success might challenge the hegemony of Piedmont, or even the

very existence of the crown. If, on the other hand, Garibaldi was captured or killed, the country would surely hold Cavour responsible. Success or failure therefore would compromise his government, and of course either event threatened him with the supreme danger of active foreign intervention in the Italian question. It is thus easily understandable why before the expedition set out Cavour should have used every means in his power to stop it. More than anything else there was the fact that he considered the idea to be a mad one, so mad indeed that probably he never seriously thought Garibaldi would sail until he had actually weighed anchor. Only when the venture had succeeded did he send help and try to control it, making a virtue out of hard necessity.

But if the Sicilian expedition upset all his own plans why then did he let it go at all? There are various answers to this. He had for one thing been assured by more persons than one that in view of the collapse of the revolt in Sicily it would not set out, and without government provision of ships, money and munitions he would have felt fairly safe that Garibaldi could not move.[8] A second com-

[7] D'Azeglio to Persano 16 July: 'I should have preferred a more open conduct rather than resorting to so many artful tricks which have deceived no-one. . . . Garibaldi went straight ahead, risking his own life, and all credit to him. Whereas we! . . . By deceit we might win something for the moment, but you lose far more in the long run when no-one can believe you any longer.' [C. di] Persano, *Diario* [*privato-politico-militare nella campagna navale 1860–1*] (2nd ed. 1869), pt. 1, p. 81.

[8] It is important to show that lack of money (which it would have been easy for the government to provide on the sly) was a serious handicap to the expedition. There were no means to buy ships, so they had to be stolen, and even then there were so many more volunteers at Genoa than ships that many people had to be sent off home again. G. Cadolini, *Memorie del*

plementary answer is that faced with such an awful decision he could not make up his mind, but let events slide, and buried his head in the sand for a fortnight while waiting for France's veto, or Garibaldi's defeat, or a miracle. Again, Cavour knew the King was both sympathetic to Garibaldi and was looking for another Prime Minister;[9] it was as much as his position was worth to defy both King and public opinion at the same time. Garibaldi's departure incidentally would have the advantage of clearing most of the hotheads out of northern Italy, away from the parliamentary battles that were threatening over Cavour's cession of Nice and Savoy to France. For there was a full-scale ministerial and parliamentary crisis at this very moment. Fanti, the Minister of War, and his most important colleague, was threatening to resign over the cessions to France, and for a time Cavour was so discouraged that he even wrote to ask if the Baron Ricasoli would think of forming a new ministry. The chief trouble was that Garibaldi was extremely popular, and the *corps diplomatique* at Turin agreed that Cavour would have fallen had he forcibly tried to stop the Thousand. Cavour himself was afraid that he might fall in any case. In all the excitement of Garibaldi's departure it has gone without observation that the expedition sailed on the very day of the parliamentary elections into which Cavour's party and Cavour himself were putting all the spare energy they had, otherwise Garibaldi might not perhaps have got away so lightly.

That these considerations were uppermost in his mind appears from letters he wrote at this time. On 12 May he wrote as follows to Nigra: 'the ministry could

not have lasted if it had tried to stop Garibaldi. With the elections on, and depending on the votes of every shade of moderate liberal to counter the opposition and get the French treaty through, I could not take strong measures to stop him. . . . At the same time I omitted nothing to persuade Garibaldi to drop his mad scheme. What with La Farina's assurances and the failure of the Sicilian insurgents, I never thought he could possibly go.'[10] On another occasion he wrote privately: 'if Garibaldi had been forcibly held back, he would have become very dangerous in internal politics.' And the

Risorgimento dal 1848 al 1862 (1911), pp. 374–6. Another of the organizers, E. Guastalla, wrote to Cadolini on 16 May that 'if we cannot get more money I do not see how we can fit out another expedition.' Cadolini Papers, in Museo del Risorgimento at Rome.

[9] Cavour to Nigra, 24 Apr.: 'j'ai lieu de croire que Sa Majesté, qui a toujours un faible pour Garibaldi, . . . cherche sous cape à m'ôter la direction des affaires.' ["I have reason to believe that His Majesty, who always has a weakness for Garibaldi, . . . is seeking undercover to remove me from the leadership of affairs."] *Cavour-Nigra*, III, 269; Cavour to Carignano, 2 May, ibid. p. 277; letter of Ricasoli to his brother Vincenzo, 29 May, *Lettere [e documenti del Barone B.] Ricasoli* (ed. Tabarrini e Gotti) v (1890), 101. Cavour never got on well with the King, but he was a little unfair to him here, for as General Türr wrote on 25 Apr. to Bertani, the King had advised the radicals to postpone the Sicilian revolt 'because for the moment it was impossible for him to make a profitable diversion in their favour.' Jessie White Mario Papers, in Museo del Risorgimento at Rome.

[10] *Cavour-Nigra*, p. 294. Cavour went on: 'I regret Garibaldi's expedition as much as anyone. . . . I could not stop him going, for force would have been necessary. . . . And the Ministry is in no position to face the immense unpopularity which would have been drawn upon it had Garibaldi been prevented. . . . As the news from Palermo showed that the state of siege there had been lifted and the revolt was on the point of being extinguished, I thought Garibaldi would be obliged to stay at home whether he liked it or not.'

public statements in his own newspaper were much the same, namely, that the government had tried every method of persuasion to stop Garibaldi, and indeed thought it had dissuaded him; according to these statements the use of force would have meant civil war, and even then might not have sufficed to stop him sailing.

Yet Cavour cannot be judged only on his own testimony, for a month later he was hinting that he had been helping all the time, and if we regard *all* his earlier statements as meant to deceive someone or other, we might twist them into a triumph of cunning and statesmanship. But the English ambassador says exactly the same, and he was closer to Cavour's real mind at the time than almost anyone else. Writing the day before the expedition sailed, Hudson said that 'if Garibaldi means to go he is sufficiently strong and sufficiently supported by public opinion to be able to go whether the government likes it or not.' And later on, in another private letter, Hudson wrote: 'at the outset nobody believed in the possibility of Garibaldi's success; and Cavour and tutti quanti [everybody] thought the country well rid of him and of the unquiet spirits who went with him. The argument was—if he fails we are rid of a troublesome fellow, and if he succeeds Italy will derive some profit from his success. Now the English ambassador had no conceivable motive for untruthfulness here. The same can be said of a confidential note written to the Minister of the Interior by the permanent secretary of his ministry, which remarks that a few hours before Garibaldi set out Cavour did agree at last to risk the use of force against him, and said that he would get Cabinet approval for it the

next morning. This is all the more likely in that a telegram would have arrived just before this from naval units in Palermo harbour to confirm that the Sicilian insurrection was at an end, so that Cavour must have thought himself at last on firmer ground. But if the story is true, he was too late in making up his mind, luckily for Italy. Or perhaps he was waiting until the election results showed that he could act without fear.[11]

After this brief sketch it may be helpful to look in more detail at a different class of evidence, and see how two or three of the facts on which is based the usual view of Cavour's benevolent intervention can fit this alternative interpretation. First of all there is the interview which Cavour had at Genoa with one of the less politically radical of Garibaldi's generals called Sirtori on 23 April, twelve days before they set out. Of this interview we have two accounts, usually said to be contradictory. Sirtori himself three years later told parliament that Cavour had offered him help if the expedition went to Sicily, but opposition if they went to the Papal States, and this statement has been taken as evidence that Cavour did actually help the Thousand. A second account of the interview was given by Bertani, also in the same parliamentary session of June 1863. Bertani told parliament how he remembered Sirtori coming back from that interview three years earlier with the story that Cavour had really said 'I don't know

---

[11] It is important to know that the elections must have been a last-minute thought by Cavour, perhaps to win support against the revolutionary activity in Genoa. Thus Depretis, the Governor of Brescia, was told only on 29 Apr. that he would have to prepare for elections on 6 May. Letter of protest of 29 Apr. from Depretis to the Minister of the Interior, in the Depretis Papers at the Archivio di Stato at Rome.

what to think or do,' though 'I believe Garibaldi will be captured.' Now which of these was right? Was Cavour helpful, or discouraging? The answer given to this tiny point may affect our larger attitude to Cavour and to one of the most fundamental controversies in *risorgimento* history. If it were a question of choosing between the two versions, Sirtori's account of Cavour's benevolence is obviously the more reliable, as first-hand evidence, even though it comes three years after the event. The Master of Trinity went so far as to conclude that no modern historian had any right to repeat Bertani's tale; though to discredit it he used a legend that Bertani had said Cavour *smiled* as he spoke of Garibaldi's probable capture, and this gives a completely altered sense to the words in question.[12] Going back again to the actual parliamentary reports, it appears that the reference to smiling must have been introduced later, and that really these parliamentary speeches were not at all the broil usually supposed, but a not unfriendly exchange, rather supplementing than contradicting each other. Bertani's statement at the time can hardly have been thought uncomplimentary to Cavour, for it was not greeted with cries of dissent like other parts of his speech. And in his very next sentence, not usually quoted, Bertani had added that if he himself had been in Cavour's shoes he would have thought exactly the same. Many other sources confirm that it was generally believed in conservative circles that Garibaldi would be captured; and, indeed, this had been one good reason why Cavour had not wanted Garibaldi to go in the first place. It is thus rather Sirtori's account which needs justification; for surely if Cavour had been really helpful

as a result of this interview we should have heard about it earlier than 1863.

Now a completely different interpretation of the interview emerges if we look on the later recollections of Sirtori and Bertani as both true in so far as they went, and then supplement them with other indirect evidence. Much more reliable, for instance, than Sirtori's memory three years later is the diary of Crispi for this very day of the interview when he was in Genoa on the spot. 'Sirtori [says this diary], while promising to assist our expedition, has great doubts of its ultimate success. And people in the confidence of Cavour are constantly coming and going in order to persuade Garibaldi to give up the idea. This confirms Bertani's statement that Cavour thought the expedition to be madness. And exactly the same conclusion is reached in a letter Crispi wrote two days after the interview, which includes this remark: 'Piedmont can give us no help. . . . We are on the point of despair.' We have other minor details which fit in with this view better than with any other: a letter by Sirtori advising Garibaldi not to move; another by Garibaldi himself explaining that the government could not help because of what he calls 'false diplomatic considerations.' As for Cavour's own testimony, he never breathed a word about having offered help in this interview. But a Cabinet minute shows that the very next day, 24 April, the ministry unani-

[12] The legend appeared in 1869 during the bitter political controversy provoked by the publication of La Farina's letters and Persano's memoirs in defence of Cavour; to which Bertani replied in an acrid polemical work which distorted history in the opposite direction. A. Bertani, *Ire politiche d'oltre tomba* (1869), p. 61. It was given more general currency in the justly popular G. Guerzoni, *Garibaldi* (1882), II, 30.

mously agreed to sequestrate the rifles which Garibaldi had stored in Milan.[13] There is little room for deceit or *arrière pensée* in a secret minute, and this fact makes it far better evidence of Cavour's intentions than remarks he made to third parties which they tried to recall three years after the event. The Cabinet decision was also followed by immediate action, for Colonel Frappolli was at once dispatched by Cavour to dissuade Garibaldi from stirring; with such cogent arguments, moreover, that he was able to report back that the expedition had been called off. These facts hardly indicate government offers of help. And finally there are the letters which Cavour wrote this same day, the 24th, to two of his ministers—and he was more likely to tell the whole truth to his own colleagues than to the revolutionary General Sirtori. These letters refer to his visit to Genoa the day before, and simply say he had there uncovered a dangerous Mazzinian agitation; he explained that he had given orders to prevent any insurrectionary movement, and added that in his opinion 'nothing serious is likely to come of it.'[14] Prof. Trevelyan points out how these two letters inexplicably contradict the interpretation he had favoured for the Sirtori interview. But the discrepancy is avoided if the affair is interpreted the other way. Cavour in Genoa recognized there was danger from Mazzini and tried to counter it, hoping to drive in still further the old wedge which separated Mazzini from Garibaldi. He was thus too prudent openly to reject this appeal from Garibaldi's chief of staff, Sirtori, especially when he knew from the Genoese authorities and from Sirtori himself that the revolt in Sicily was collapsing and the expedition unlikely to set out in any case.

Help, therefore, might be offered with impunity. His principal fear was lest Garibaldi should revert from his forlorn hope in Sicily and instead attack the Papal States through Tuscany, so destroying the credit of Piedmont with France. Accordingly he spoke fair words, hoping thereby to retain some influence over Garibaldi, hinting therefore at possible government help if he behaved himself and kept to his Sicilian plan, but insisting chiefly on the chances of unsuccess and the inadvisability of precipitate action.[15] Sirtori then would have come

[13] 24 Apr.: 'it was unanimously decided to refuse Garibaldi the guns he requires for the Sicilian insurrection, lest the European capitals should thereby be alarmed, in view of the imprudent publicity given by him and his friends in Genoa to the preparations he has in hand for Sicily. It was also resolved that any meeting of the emigrés in Genoa should be forbidden.' It may be significant that no further entry in the minute book is recorded until after Garibaldi had set out on 8 May. The important fact that these Minutes were not only private but almost personal to Cavour is suggested by the fact that he was the first to introduce the idea of Cabinet minutes, and that they were discontinued during the intervening ministry. *Copia di verbali delle adunanze del Consiglio dei Ministri tenuta per uso del Conte di Cavour*, Archivio di Stato, Rome.

[14] *Cavour-Nigra*, III, 266, letter to Farini. The other letter, to Nigra, remarked that 'je soupçonne le Roi de favoriser imprudemment ces projets. J'ai donné l'ordre de surveiller et d'empêcher si cela est possible ces tentatives désespérées' ["I suspect the King of imprudently favoring these projects. I have issued an order for surveillance and for prevention, if this is possible, of these desperate attempts"] (ibid. p. 269). On 23 Apr. he had written to Nigra (ibid. p. 264): 'le Gouvernement du Roi fait des efforts pour empêcher Garibaldi d'aller en Sicile, je ne sais pas si l'on réussira' ['The Royal Government is taking measures to prevent Garibaldi from going to Sicily, but I do not know if they will be successful.']

[15] There is a significant difference of wording in an account which Sirtori himself gave closer to the event in a letter to Conti Giulini of 3 May: 'what Cavour then said to me led us to hope for

back from this meeting and told people of Cavour's pessimism which he himself fully shared, and it would have been naturally this impression which remained uppermost in Bertani's mind. Whereas Sirtori, in happy retrospect after he had received military preferment at Cavour's hands, recalled rather the fair words, mistakenly associating with those words the concrete help which Cavour gave six weeks later in different circumstances.

So much for the *nihil obstat* ["no objection"] which Cavour is supposed to have given on 23 April to the Sicilian exploit. A second controversial point which should next be considered is the sequestration of the 12,000 firearms at Milan. These arms belonged to Garibaldi's party, but the government was storing them at one of its own arsenals in order that some check might be imposed on the use to which they were put. Since until this moment the authorities had allowed freedom of withdrawal unless Garibaldi should act against Cavour's wishes, refusal at this moment of all moments therefore suggested that Garibaldi's proposed expedition was disapproved by the government. It was on 16 April that Garibaldi sent for the withdrawal of a mere 200 rifles from the store, and to his surprise was refused by the Governor of Milan, D'Azeglio. D'Azeglio took full responsibility for this himself, but wrote off at once to Farini, the Minister of the Interior, asking him to confirm the refusal. No reply came from the minister, and a week later D'Azeglio had to write again to Turin pressing for an answer; in these circumstances the minister's silence was rightly assumed at Milan to be tantamount to the desired confirmation. Meanwhile Farini, though fully

competent as Minister of the Interior to give orders to his subordinate governors, had passed the matter to Cavour, and Cavour had passed it back again.[16] Neither wanted to commit himself, and yet each must have realized that silence would merely save his own reputation at the price of leaving Garibaldi disarmed and helpless. In fact the minutes of the Cabinet already quoted show that the ministry, including Cavour whose actual signature they bear, were unanimous in approving D'Azeglio's action; though their approval was kept secret, and Cavour still went on letting D'Azeglio take and keep responsibility for the matter, knowing he could then disown his subordinate's action if things turned out badly. Cavour's excuse was that at all costs it had to appear as if the government was not conniving; and this excuse, if correct, would at least prove that the motive of 'not being compromised' ranked higher with him than that of 'giving secret help.' But if he really wished to help short of being compromised, as his apologists declare, he could have told D'Azeglio privately to disobey his official command; a discreet order to disobey orders was not unknown later in 1860. The excuse was obviously a mere pretext, for Cavour was bound to be compromised if Garibaldi sailed, whereas the permission for arms to be withdrawn from government arsenals had been given before now with-

---

help from him.' N. Bianchi, *Storia documentata della diplomazia europea in Italia*, VIII (1872), 290.

[16] Borromeo to Farini, 24 Apr., and Farini to Cavour, 27 Apr., in Farini Papers. Borromeo told Farini that Cavour left the decision entirely to him: 'Count Cavour, to whom I referred the question of Garibaldi's rifles, would like you to give instructions on the convenience or otherwise of the request made by Garibaldi that he should be allowed to withdraw some of them.'

out disaster. The more immediate fear which possessed Cavour was that of throwing away good money on a desperate venture which was unlikely to succeed, and which if it did succeed would benefit his political opponents. There will always, no doubt, be some scope for difference of opinion over what it might have been diplomatically possible for Cavour to do by way of help, because the answer to such a question depends on one's interpretation of human nature as well as on inescapable inferences from documents; but financial help was surely easy, and he gave none. The Thousand were forced to set out with a few rusty, smooth-bore, converted flintlocks, the only advantage of which was that they imposed a tactic of bayonet charges which effectively struck terror into the Neapolitan soldiery.[17] Only over a month later when Palermo had fallen did the government allow these new Enfield rifles out of bond.

A third point which ought to be discussed is the alleged protection given to the Thousand by the Piedmontese fleet under Admiral Persano. One of the foundations for this allegation is an almost certainly apocryphal document wherein Cavour is said to have told Persano to cruise between Garibaldi and the Neapolitan fleet, adding: 'I hope you understand me.' Only with much stretching can this be made to seem like an order to protect the expedition, but in any case we have but one oblique reference to the existence of this document, and Trevelyan is right not to mention it. The known facts point rather the other way. On 3 May Persano was ordered to leave Tuscany and cruise near Sardinia, where Garibaldi's route would most likely lie. There is evidence that on 5 May Cavour

was at last resolved to use force; and this resolution must have been confirmed when Garibaldi first landed not in Sicily but in Tuscany, which terrified Cavour with the prospect of an invasion of the Papal States, and also gave him the excuse he had so far lacked to win round public opinion against such folly. Then on 7 May the election returns showed that he would have a large parliamentary majority and so could act. Cavour's actual order now was that Persano should arrest Garibaldi if he touched at any Sardinian port but not if he was encountered in the open sea. The customary interpretation of this has been that it was not intended seriously but was another clever ruse to deceive European diplomacy. It is, however, hardly likely that Cavour would have run the risk of deceiving his own admiral too. Persano at once wired for personal confirmation of such an important order, and the reply came back that 'the Ministry' had decided for Garibaldi's arrest. Now nine years later when Persano published his Memoirs he interpreted this to mean that Cavour personally had been against the other ministers—in other words had hoped that Persano would see through the wording of the telegram and disobey. But one must remember that nine years later everyone knew that Garibaldi had been successful, and the exigencies of party politics made it necessary to justify Cavour in that respect. If, instead, one looks at things as they appeared in 1860 it is surely unthinkable that Persano could have done anything else but arrest Garibaldi had he shown his face in port.

[17] Of these weapons, given by the National Society, it was 'no exaggeration to say that nine out of ten would not fire at all'—note by Garibaldi in G. E. Curàtulo, *Garibaldi, Vittorio Emanuele, Cavour* (1911), p. 177.

Besides this there are still other difficulties in the story. It would, for instance, be unique if Cavour had let himself be overruled on such a matter by his own Cabinet. Of course it is always probable that he was still unable to make up his mind, and was trying not to commit himself in writing, hoping, for instance, that Persano, like D'Azeglio and Garibaldi before him, would take action on his own responsibility one way or the other, ready to be disowned if necessary. Actually the confirmatory order reached Persano too late for him to be able to do much about it; though nine years later, when he had to explain how Garibaldi's two little boats had eluded the vigilance of His Majesty's navy, he rationalized the matter as an example of his own astuteness and Cavour's cunning. Garibaldi for his part, in reviewing the Admiral's Memoirs, recollected that when Persano arrived in Sicily later in May 1860 'he assured me that he had had orders to follow and arrest me; and if he did not carry them out, it was because luckily our expedition, instead of coasting Sardinia as we had first planned, was switched via Tuscany by unforeseen circumstances, and so escaped the claws of the Piedmontese fleet.' This version does certainly fit better with what we know of Cavour's other statements at the time, and can only be gainsaid if we assume that all his public and private pronouncements were without exception deceitful. He repeated his orders for Garibaldi's arrest to other people like Ricasoli and Prince Carignano in Tuscany, and he could not think that all these would see through any deception there may have been. On 11 May he went so far as to order that Garibaldi should be arrested anywhere he could be found outside Si-

cilian waters; and all expeditions to reinforce him were to be prevented at all costs—the words 'at all costs' were underlined and repeated in more telegrams than one.

The conclusion then must be that Cavour played a less important and less happy part than often thought in the movement which conquered half Italy from the Bourbons. The facts only fit together if we assume, first, that there was a kind of hiatus in his policy; and secondly, that on balance he did more initially to hinder than to help the conquest of Sicily. In fact his chief merit was that he did not absolutely veto the expedition, and it may be argued that even in this respect his attitude was one which was forced upon him.

We need not raise the question whether Cavour is to be blamed for lack of courage or vision. We shall be safe to consider that he could probably have done little else, and we must admire the great skill with which he retrieved the situation later, and reasserted his influence over events. It is not likely that history will shake Cavour's position in the very front rank of nineteenth-century statesmen: but this makes it all the more necessary to have a just appraisal of his talents and his limitations, and a better appreciation of the nature of statesmanship itself.

In May 1860 his position was almost impossibly difficult. He was confronted with elections and a ministerial crisis together, with all the worry of having to pilot through parliament the unpopular surrender of Nice and Savoy. Public opinion seemed to be leaving him for the more picturesque Garibaldi; while Garibaldi's success threatened to ruin his foreign policy and bring incalculable dangers to Italy. So, short of using force, he did his best to thwart the revolutionaries, though in the last resort he had not the courage or the strength to prevent them setting out, and in self-defence was compelled to allow something he inwardly regarded as a misfortune. He had weighed up the chances of success but had made a mistake in his calculations, and had his advice been followed southern Italy would not have fallen when it did. Cavour did not usually lack daring, but on this occasion the suddenness of events threw him out of his equilibrium. Far from helping Garibaldi while cleverly appearing not to (which is the traditional view), it seems that he gave no help while cleverly appearing as if he might do so at any moment. In reality he had no intention of squandering government resources on a buccaneering exploit that bid fair to ruin his own career and reputation. Even on a less severe interpretation of his motives, he was determined to avoid anything that might compromise him or be regarded as taking sides at least until one or other of the combatants had actually won. In fact, he had the worst of both worlds, for Piedmont was inevitably compromised without having been able to exert herself adequately for the cause. What was more, the rift between Cavour and Garibaldi now became unbridgeable. Not only were the two chief architects of Italian unity to be brought more than once within appreciable distance of civil war, but even after a lapse of ninety years the bitterness thereby injected into Italian politics has barely yet had time to disappear.

* * *

People are generally agreed that the worry of southern Italy, and of Gari-

baldi's angry, wounding remarks in parliament, were among the contingent causes of Cavour's death. But he died at the very highest point of his success, a few weeks after the existence of a kingdom of Italy had been officially proclaimed and parliament had given him another overwhelming vote of confidence. The heroic age of the *risorgimento* was just ending, and his own name was not to be associated with the prosaic years to come.

By Cavour's own confession the methods he had employed were often irregular. Not for nothing did he acknowledge his debt to Machiavelli as a master of statecraft. His adaptability and tactical resource had proved quite astounding. He had been flexible enough to realize that Mazzini's concept of national unity was more practicable than he had once thought, and he had then outbidden the radicals in his zeal, and outplayed them at their own game of revolution. At the very moment when he seemed most helpless between France on one side and the advancing army of Italian volunteers on the other, he had with exquisite tact threatened Napoleon with Garibaldi, and Garibaldi with Napoleon; so doing, he had neutralized both of them, and had himself intervened as a *tertius gaudens* [a third party who benefits from the quarrels of others] to inherit the Papal States from one and the whole of southern Italy from the other. He was not content with this. At the very same moment he was sending arms to Hungary, in case he needed a revolution there, either to check an Austrian invasion or to help win Venice. He was even considering the preliminary moves for annexing Trieste, knowing that 'we must sow so that our children may reap.'

All this was a fine example of resourceful opportunism. Armed at all points, most fertile in expedient, he seized and concentrated on every weakness in his opponents: on Garibaldi's *faible* [weakness] for Victor Emanuel, on Rattazzi's ambition for power, on the prevalent dread of revolution, on British suspicion of France, and on the fact that Napoleon could neither join with Britain nor oppose her. These were all exploited to good effect. In his treatment of the radicals he knew that they would sacrifice themselves and pay any cost so that Italy became a unified nation. With the conservatives he had to tread more delicately, for his cession to France of their stronghold in Savoy had been a bitter blow. This was no doubt one reason why another *connubio* [political marriage] with the parliamentary Left could only have weakened him. He could rely on the grudging support of the radicals as soon as he accepted their nationalist programme; but he had to win the conservatives at the price of a breach with Garibaldi, by ending the revolution and extending their power throughout the length and breadth of Italy.

Cavour's success had much that was paradoxical about it. Somehow he managed to persuade people to back a revolution on the excuse that this was the way to prevent revolution. He and the whole moderate party had first to swallow the unpalatable doctrines of universal suffrage and popular sovereignty which they abhorred. He found himself justifying a monarchy established 'by will of the people,' and the right of rebellion against a regularly constituted government. In the process he had brought good Catholics to the point where they cheerfully sang Te Deums for the invasion of the Papal States. Liberals had likewise been softened until they thought nothing of harsh repression of the opposition press, and countenancing arbitrary arrest without trial. Southerners, who had rebelled in great part because they wanted to be rid of the excessive centralization of government in the city of Naples, had to accept and like an even greater dependence upon remoter Turin. Not least in difficulty, the king had to be in appearance a constitutional king, that is to say he had to do what Cavour wanted, at the same time as he went on thinking himself the real master in charge.

On close inspection Cavour and Garibaldi become—probably like most people—at once greater and lesser than first appearances had suggested; and it was in their least generous and least perceptive side, namely their hostile attitude to each other, that they found one of the mainsprings of action with which to create a unitary state. Upon the tension between these two the fate of Italy for a time depended. If Garibaldi renounced caution and set out for Sicily, a decisive consideration with him was his fury at Cavour's sale of Nice, and his conviction that the government could not be stimulated to remedial action except under the stress of imminent danger. When, later on, he sailed across the Straits to Naples, this was partly so that he might defy the French in Rome, and so overturn the Napoleonic alliance upon which Cavour relied. If Cavour then invaded the Marches, this was because he was frightened that the revolution would reach Rome and even penetrate his own kingdom of Sardinia. In January 1861, Cavour apparently still considered the 'struggle against Garibaldianism' to be his main task.

The two men were temperamentally as well as politically antipathetic. To see how deep a rift lay between them, and how ineffective were the attempts to bridge it, one must reach behind the sentimental legends of later official history. Some people have professed to see no evidence at all that Cavour 'was either hostile, or uncertain, or treacherous in his actions towards the revolutionary forces under Garibaldi,' and to find no support for the theory 'that he was ready to make use of them first and then throw them on one side.' The contention of this present book has been almost precisely the opposite. Cavour was sometimes treacherous, often uncertain, and always more or less hostile to Garibaldi; and indeed one can almost say that he was *necessarily* all of these things. The rift between them, it is true, was deliberately widened by arrogant diehards on both sides, chief among them La Farina and Bertani, who had too little charity and vision to know what they were doing. It was also exploited by Rattazzi's party at Turin, who used it as an argument for saying that Cavour must resign; and this forced Cavour into opposing Garibaldi the more relentlessly as an enemy of parliamentary government. But fundamentally it represented just the natural division between Left and Right, between rashness and caution, radicalism and conservatism, between the method of the sword and the method of diplomacy. One side believed in all or nothing, while the other saw the value of circumlocution and gradualism. Yet both were necessary for the making of Italy.

Cavour was too clever and too practical a man to be very consistent in his attitude towards the revolution. He had begun by looking on Garibaldi's expedition as reckless folly, doomed to failure like that of the Bandiera brothers several years before. Then he became frightened that it would succeed too well, that it would spoil his own scheme of gradual expansion by Piedmont under the benevolent protection of Napoleonic France. There were some moments when he was afraid that Garibaldi was a puppet of the republicans; others when he feared that the radical leader was representing dictatorial against parliamentary government; at other moments his was just an aristocratic contempt for an uneducated man, for a vulgar soldier who was too big for his boots and with whom one could not carry on ordinary relations as with a responsible adult. Sometimes Garibaldi was to be feared as someone who might betray the monarchy, at other times as someone who was too good a monarchist to be a good parliamentarian, someone to whom the monarchy might owe too much. At all times, however, Cavour was superbly self-confident that he himself was the only man to be trusted with affairs of state. Neither Garibaldi, nor any other person in Italy, Ricasoli and the king included, should in his view have the power of independent initiative, or else disaster would follow.

Not even the events of 1860 were to shake this self-confidence; indeed they only increased it. For four months Cavour had had to submit to a succession of failures, first in not being able to stop Garibaldi leaving for Sicily, then in not being able to annex the island after the fall of Palermo, then in La Farina and Depretis failing to tame Garibaldi and prevent him crossing the straits to reach Naples as a conqueror. Up to this point

Cavour had played a much less important and much less happy part than is often thought in the movement which conquered half Italy from the Bourbons. He had done more to hinder than to help, basing himself on a bad miscalculation about the political forces at work and the readiness of Italy for nationhood. But finally he had managed to reassert his influence triumphantly over events. He had successfully arrested Garibaldi's advance on Rome, and had ensured the triumph of liberal and centralized monarchy over all the other radical and federalist alternatives put forward by his opponents.

The contribution of the radicals to Italian unification cannot usefully be measured against Cavour's. In his more magnanimous moments Cavour had the perception to see that the radicals were invaluable, even though he had been compelled to discard them like orange peel—to use Garibaldi's expression. The failure of Cavour's party to win or even to start a revolution in either Palermo or Naples is the best indication of what Italy owed to the revolutionaries. Cavour was wont to look upon them as unpractical ideologues; but the real ideologues were rather the moderate liberals in Sicily and Naples who talked and did little but await the issue of events; not the perhaps extravagant thinkers who acted and bore the burden and heat of the day's labour. The moderates could not easily forgive their own failure to rise and deliver themselves, and this did not make them take any more kindly to being liberated by people they called 'thieves' and 'assassins.' But one must remember that the very word 'moderate' was often claimed merely for propaganda purposes by people who were bigots in their moderation, and who were sometimes a match for any extremists in violence of language. They are often better described as 'conservatives.' They were trimmers, sometimes for worthy, sometimes for unworthy motives, people who lacked strong views and clearness of aim, people who for the most part lacked drive, fire and audacity. Italy owed them a great deal, but not everything.

It was Garibaldi, Crispi and Bertani who took on themselves the principal risk and responsibility of failure over this revolution in the south. These radical enthusiasts would have been mercilessly killed had they failed, and as mercilessly condemned by Italians and by history. As events turned out, it was their misfortune to be blamed even for their success. Cavour was always quite ready to disown them, and indeed he even expected to do so; and they knew as much and were content. Looking ahead to Aspromonte and Mentana one can see what might easily have happened in 1860. Cavour's successors twice allowed or incited Garibaldi to risk his life and the future of Italy, but subsequently had to order their troops to fire upon and wound him, to arrest him and his men, and then to cover him with the obloquy of failure. This was what Garibaldi knowingly risked again and again. If he had been ambitious for himself, his conduct would not have been so admirable; but he was in everything unostentatious, not least in his graceful surrender of office in November; and when in April 1861 Musolino proposed in parliament to make him a gift from the nation, this proposal had to be withdrawn at Garibaldi's own wish. If he had not dutifully obeyed the king, this too would have made him lack something of greatness. But he was as loyal in obedience as he was resolute in command. There were many of the trappings of vulgar dictatorship about him; and yet one must not leave out of account how he impressed men of intellect as well as of action with his claims to be considered a liberal and essentially a good man.

Garibaldi's chief service to his country in 1860 was as a fighter. He still remains probably the greatest Italian general of modern times. He had a fine instinct for strategy, and a better grasp on most elements of the art of war than his critics have often allowed. The regular generals derided his contempt for passwords and uniforms and punitive discipline; but when all is said and done, it needed very remarkable teamwork and leadership to raise and provide for forty thousand soldiers, and his great enthusiasm and will-to-win brought Italy her finest military victories of the whole *risorgimento*.

As a civil governor Garibaldi suffered from being unintelligent, inexperienced and prone to take bad advice; but when he really turned his attention to a point, one cannot help being impressed with what Marc Monnier called his 'rare bon sens qui lui tient lieu de science et d'art politique' [rare good sense which makes up for his lack of political science and skill.'] As an administrator he does not compare so very unfavourably with Farini, who had far greater experience, far greater resources, and no military distractions to take away his attention. Despite the arrogant conviction of the moderates that they were the only repository of political wisdom and skill, it seems that Sicily was more anarchical after Montezemolo than after Mordini. In May 1860 the good sense and right political instincts of Garibaldi had served Italy better than the wiles of Cavour. In June and afterwards it was his resistance to Cavour's policy of immediate annexation which made possible the acquisition of central and southern Italy. And finally, looking back in the light of later events, it is not so clear now as it was to Cavour that annexation was better obtained by plebiscite alone without the aid of a consultative assembly.

Garibaldi had an instinctive understanding of some southern problems, an understanding which often escaped observers in the north. Unlike the Piedmontese conservatives, for instance, he had the good sense to see that Mazzini presented no danger to law and order in Naples, except perhaps in so far as the 'moderates' might stir up popular riots against him. Garibaldi understood both Mazzini and the south better than Cavour ever did, for the same reason that he had much more knowledge of and sympathy with the common people. Instead of assuming that southerners were idle and corrupt, and instead of trying to impose a cut-and-dried system upon them, he had worked by appealing to their good nature; and this had evoked a far more positive response than greeted his more technically efficient successors. What he gave them was enthusiasm, faith in a cause, and a fine example of self-sacrifice and courage. These were the very qualities which Mazzini all along had said were necessary for making Italians conscious of their strength, for making them politically conscious and politically responsible. Mazzini's chief objection to the Cavourian system was that it did not start by teaching the nation an awareness of its nationhood, and did not go on to persuade the common people that they ought to co-operate in building their own nation. The party of Cavour was in general ignorant and frightened of the common people, and preferred to impose its will with the aid of diplomacy, rather than to rouse this sleeping giant and give it ideas above its station.

Once again here was evidence of the sheer practicality of the radical idealists. By comparison, the stolid opposition of southern peasants in 1861 was to show the essential unpracticality of the hard-headed men who worked more by calculation and 'interest.' In comparing the liberal with the radical method, one must first remember that diplomacy exacted a price, Savoy and Nice in exchange for Tuscany; and as a second point, that the radicals in southern Italy had proved the common people to be a superb initiating force. In the eyes of the populace Garibaldi was a hero who brought out the best in them. He stood for all that seemed good in the *risorgimento,* all that was heroic, romantic, honest, and 'popular' in the sense of 'of the people'; while Cavour, for all his skill and success, stood for many of its worst aspects, for what was matter-of-fact, for duplicity, lack of generosity, for shady bargains with Louis Napoleon, and all that was double-faced and deceitful. Early in 1861 some of the deputies had to conclude that Garibaldi would not have been so bad after all as a royal viceroy in the south; and though historians have usually ridiculed Garibaldi's offer to take this post, he could hardly have done much worse than Farini and most of his many successors. At least there would probably have been a more friendly and enthusiastic spirit in Naples and Sicily. People would not so easily have been able to say afterwards that the great majority of Italian citizens were quite detached from, and uninterested in, the movement for national independence.

ETTORE PASSERIN d'ENTRÈVES (1914–   ),
professor of *Risorgimento* history at Milan's Catholic
University, has written a series of essays on Cavour's
"last political battle." Although the collection deals
chiefly with events in the first half of 1861, some
passages are designed to serve as a gentle reply to
Mack Smith's rather harsh appraisal of Cavour's
behavior toward Garibaldi and the south. Passerin
d'Entrèves' book rests on examination of the recently
published correspondence by Cavour on the Southern
Question that Mack Smith used and some additional
documents. His conclusion is that the countermoves
taken by the Cavourian moderates against
Garibaldi were historically justified.*

Cavour's Countermoves Justified

The publication of Denis Mack Smith's long-awaited study on the conflict between Cavour and Garibaldi, the two protagonists of Italian nationalist policy in 1860, impels us to try to understand better how Piedmont's hegemonic policy, which so quickly became the subject of many bitter denunciations, actually manifested itself between 1860 and 1861.

It can certainly be said that the treaty ceding to France the old transalpine provinces of Savoy and Nice—an action denounced by the democrats as vile trafficking in peoples—in a sense marked the end of the old Savoyard-Piedmontese dynastic state and laid the basis for the final effort at unification. . . . Writing to [Costantino] Nigra, his trusted friend [in Paris], toward the end of July [1860], Cavour declared that Garibaldi's expedition [to Sicily] was decided upon or stimulated by the cession of Nice, and that the new impetuosity of the Italian national movement resulted from the abrupt [armistice of] Villafranca. . . .

In the same letter Cavour emphasized the grave political difficulties in which he was ever more deeply involved as a result of the cession of the transalpine provinces. Not even within his own cab-

* From Ettore Passerin d'Entrèves, *L'ultima battaglia politica di Cavour: I problemi dell'unificazione italiana* (Turin: Industria Libraria Tipografica Editrice, 1956), pp. 72-83, omitting the original footnotes. Translated by Charles F. Delzell. Reprinted by permission of the author and Industria Libraria Tipografica Editrice.

inet had he found unanimous support, because he had to take into account a certain reluctance on the part of War Minister- Fanti to accept the new boundary. The results of the cession were even graver when it came to parliamentary division. In Cavour's judgment, it led to a noticeable weakening of the majority's position—so much so as to prevent him from halting Garibaldi's expedition to Sicily, which departed at the critical moment in discussions of the treaty that was signed on March 24, [1860]. . . . Outside of Parliament, in the more radical sectors of patriotic opinion, protests were even livelier. Cavour realized, for example, how the cession of Nice could arouse violent repercussions in the soul of Garibaldi, and he foresaw to a certain extent the painful polemics that would erupt in April 1861. . . .

The creativeness in Cavour's policy must be seen within the framework of his having to make practical decisions. Certainly all the resistance he set up against Garibaldi's audacious steps [in the south] in the summer of 1860 was in behalf of a conservative program. The essential features of this program were the primacy of monarchical Piedmont's initiative over the revolutionary one; preservation of the central nucleus of the Papal States in order to forestall an open breach with France; and prevention of any step toward a republican and democratic regime that would be unpopular in the eyes of Europe, including England. But it is also true that Cavour's action corresponded perfectly to the logic of that famous liberal *juste-milieu*[1] which since his youth he had considered to be his own political creed.

At the beginning of August [1860], when he was frightened by the success of "Garibaldi's adventures," Cavour went so far as to play the role of conspirator in [Bourbon-held] Naples along with a small group of refugees and some anti-Bourbon liberals. He adopted a rather ambiguous method, but the goal he pursued was not in the least ambiguous. Whoever keeps in mind the dangers that Cavour faced and the reefs on which Garibaldi's policy might crash within the span of a few months will not wish to attribute too negative an interpretation to this episode. Fully sensing the Italian destiny of the House of Savoy and the Piedmontese State (which had been vaguely perceived by some old Savoyard diplomats and theorized later in [Vincenzo] Gioberti's *Del Rinnovamento civile d'Italia* [1851]), Cavour had decisively broken away from the strictly regional "artichoke policy."[2] This is shown by his reliance on the force of national opinion, his surrounding himself with non-Piedmontese collaborators, and his fearless gambling where not a single cautious statesman of any other Italian state would have dared to do so.

In August 1860 Cavour's disciple, Nigra, wrote to him from Paris that it was not necessary to run to meet Garibaldi but rather to halt him, and to do so with the help of all the moderately liberal opinion that had its stronghold in Parliament. Nigra suggested the possibility of a cabinet crisis, of a third Novara,[3] and of a salvage *in extremis,* as possible ways out of the distressing dilemmas that had emerged the moment Garibaldi set himself up as the symbol of a democratic triumph, albeit within the

---

[1] Golden mean.—*Ed.*

[2] Slow whittling away of territory belonging to Piedmont's neighbors.—*Ed.*

[3] Another Piedmontese military defeat.—*Ed.*

framework of the national monarchy. It would no longer be possible to preserve the prestige of a monarch who was reduced to being merely the "friend of Garibaldi," or to persuade him to accept the crown of the Italian Kingdom from the hands of a popular *condottiero*. But the appeal to Parliament that Nigra recommended had a trace of doctrinaire utopianism. A liberal Parliament that dared to outlaw the victorious leader of an enterprise that was arousing the keenest enthusiasm among patriots throughout Italy would forever disqualify itself as an organ of liberal and national opinion. The most that one could still envisage would be a hegemonic program on the part of moderate liberals in a *northern kingdom*—and this would mean abandoning the south to Garibaldian "anarchy" and eventual foreign intervention by either the French or the Austrians.

At this moment Cavour made his most audacious choice and thereby clearly disproved the Mazzinian allegation (of 1858) that he was looking only to the north and not to Italy. With full awareness of the dangers still to be faced, Cavour sought "to strip from Garibaldi's hands the supreme command of the national movement" (to use his own words). Thus from the moment that the need for national unification assumed in the opinion of Cavour and his government the value and dignity of a goal to which everything else must be subordinated, one can no longer speak simply of a dynastic and Piedmontese policy.

In order to make Italy at the present time [Cavour replied to Nigra], it is not necessary to set Victor Emmanuel against Garibaldi. Garibaldi has great moral power, and he enjoys immense prestige not only in Italy but especially in Europe. You are wrong, in my opinion, in saying that we find ourselves between Garibaldi and Europe. If I were to enter into a struggle with Garibaldi tomorrow, it is likely that I would have the majority of the old diplomats on my side, but European public opinion would be against me, and public opinion would be right, for Garibaldi has rendered the greatest service to Italy that a man can give.

Thus Cavour was able to reply to collaborators like Nigra who saw Piedmont already "outlawed by Europe," not merely by the conservative sector of Europe. For even Napoleon III, who was clearly opposed to a unified Italy, threatened a break, and liberal England frowned when the Italian policy of nationalism became aggressive with respect to Austria. Moreover, Cavour was able to resist the pseudo-democratic alternatives proposed to him by such men as [Bettino] Ricasoli and [Vincenzo] Salvagnoli. It is enough to scan the important letters published recently with respect to August and September 1860 to see that even the liberals who were best trained and were capable of making serene political judgments nearly always lacked the sense of balance which enabled Cavour simultaneously to accept and to reject Garibaldi's initiative and to work his way out of the difficult situation without serious inconsistencies. Certain false moves at that time could have proved fatal to liberal principles as well as to such institutions of the Piedmontese-Italian State as the monarchy, the army, and Parliament, which had to remain the cornerstones of the edifice under construction. Even Ricasoli, who feared that the monarchy would be contaminated by contact with "revolution" and who was ready to crack down harshly on any *unorthodox* patriotic faction, did not believe that he was weakening himself by granting *carte blanche* to [Giovanni] Nicotera and other potential invaders of the Papal States in July–August 1860, for he remained obsessed by the scandal of the pope's temporal power, a power that ever since June he had wished to "annihilate," "soon, completely, and forever."

Toward the end of August, Cavour could well reply to the impatient: "I have a clear conscience that I have done everything that can be done to assist the Italian movement. Certainly one could not and ought not to play the role of a revolutionary in Sicily. But because revolution was indispensable for the overthrow of the Bourbons, I not only let it be carried out but supported it." Thus he distinguished between the advisability of promoting a revolution from abroad and the danger of promoting revolution from within the boundaries of the state in question. For this reason he pleasantly reminded Ricasoli how much the verdict of the parliamentary majority meant for himself:

If Parliament, which is to reconvene shortly, should decide that we have not displayed the energy and audacity that the times require, we should willingly surrender our position to men who represent more advanced ideas and less considerate proposals. Such men could make an appeal to revolution without betraying their antecedents and losing their reputation. But so long as power remains in our hands, we have the clear obligation to prevent the standard of revolution from flying alongside that of the King and the country. . . . The slightest act of weakness could ruin us. . . . While we dissolve the irregular and illegal corps of volunteers, we are issuing orders to organize the mobile National Guard, in which the volunteers will find a place. But we want the mobile National Guard to carry the same banner as the Army, and we do not want it to be led by such open foes of the monarchy as Nicotera.

What seemed most ambiguous and Machiavellian in the changing attitude of Cavour's policy, formulated amid extraordinary difficulties during that memorable summer of 1860, was his continuous shifting to new positions with respect to Garibaldi. After the [latter's] success in Calabria, Cavour telegraphed Admiral Persano and Villamarina on August 30 to quit trying to establish in Naples any kind of government hostile to Garibaldi (such as [Cavour] had wished to do up until the 27th) but rather to "achieve a frank agreement with him." There was certainly no cynical basis for this complete reversal, however, as is proved by the letter Cavour wrote Garibaldi on August 31—a letter that was a generously "outstretched hand," save for certain nonexplicit reservations due to a different political perspective, and this was certainly no *fault*. After all, even Garibaldi concealed some of his aims at the moment when he was negotiating with allies of the moderate faction!

In reality, it was Garibaldi's entry into the Bourbon capital [of Naples] on September 7 that marked the beginning of a period of paradoxical complications and ideological contaminations. What was revealed then was not Cavour's error but the nonexistence of any Garibaldian political line whatever, as well as the ambiguous nature of the ultrademocratic policy which, because of its moralistic intransigence, Garibaldi sought to substitute for Cavour's *opportunistic* program. By agreeing to enter Naples almost under the auspices of the famous Liborio Romano,[4] even though this was done to

[4] A defecting police official in the Bourbon capital.—*Ed.*

prevent bitter struggle, Garibaldi was adopting for himself the program of the *napoletanisti*[5]—a program of "changing nothing," of preserving the collapsing political and social structure of the former kingdom, and eliminating only the Bourbon dynasty. [Radicals like] Bertani, Crispi, and Cattaneo became shadows without bodies once [Garibaldi] agreed to this compromise with *napoletanismo*. Yet it would have been quite difficult [for him] to act otherwise, with a Bourbon army still strong along the Volturno River, and with a "frightful revolutionary minority" in Naples.

Actually the victory of the unification program in Naples was almost illusory. In the face of the ever more apparent deficiencies of *garibaldismo*, there was no other force capable of dominating the situation in the south. This was the situation that confronted Cavour when he carried out his extremely audacious act of dispatching an expedition into Umbria and the Marches. The two rival forces which hitherto had stimulated one another and had converged in the liberation of the south and in the elimination of the Bourbon dynasty now found themselves faced with problems that not even a joint enterprise could resolve. But such a joint enterprise was impossible, and this made the situation almost hopeless, at least for several months. This tragic aspect of the climactic, decisive phase of the struggle for unification has remained covered up by official historiography, which has drawn a veil over the mistakes and deficiencies of the *victors* and shown little interest in the state of mind of the *defeated*. In this regard and within these limitations, we can make use of some portions of the well-informed though extremely tendentious interpreta-

tion by Mack Smith of the period in question.

In September 1860 the political tension between Cavour's program and that of the democrats reached maximum intensity with Garibaldi's ultimatum to King Victor Emmanuel to rid himself of his *bad* ministers, and with the first evidence that there was *state-wide* opposition in the former Kingdom of the Two Sicilies to Cavour and Piedmont. . . . [Quite] promising for the democrats was a development in the continental portion of the ex-Kingdom, where a whole complex of sentiments, interests, and wounded feelings was consolidating into a common opposition bloc to Cavour and Piedmont. The emergence of this opposition front is a most interesting phenomenon to anyone who wishes to study the political activity of Cavour's government between October 1860 and May 1861. This opposition front thought it was still dealing with the old Piedmont and the old dynastic policy of the House of Savoy—in short, with an archaic world that must be rejected. In reality, however, it stood face to face with new and living political forces. Unless one indulges in a Manichaean-type judgment regarding political good and evil or progressive and reactionary forces, one cannot minimize the *morality*, experience, and potentiality of these new forces and assert that they were merely servile instruments of an archaic world.

Consciously or otherwise, Mack Smith underestimates an entire series of testimonies which tend to confirm the coherency and the *logicality* of Cavour's policy, despite all its changeableness, during the summer of 1860. He has made his own personal selection from the docu-

[5] The Naples-oriented political faction within the Bourbon Kingdom.—*Ed.*

ments and has deliberately excluded those that might negate his general line of interpretation, as is easy to see if one glances through Cavour's correspondence or, better yet, becomes acquainted with the unpublished sources on which the English scholar relies. . . . By reading [some of the unpublished letters] by the democratic foes of Cavour, [one] can easily judge the rather abstract character of their objections, which were inspired by a patriotic, mystical, moralistic puritanism that was still very close to that Mazzinian outlook, which impinged with such difficulty on some features of the intricate reality of interests and forces that were in competition. And then by reading the no less interesting criticisms set forth by the Neapolitan *municipalisti* faction and the learned but politically ignorant [economist, Francesco] Ferrara, one will be in a position to evaluate with greater equanimity certain harsh stands taken by the Piedmontese premier.

Mack Smith has relied especially on those chapters of the beautiful biography which the English republican, Jessie White Mario, dedicated to the noble figure of Agostino Bertani, and which refer to the "accusations of Cavour against Garibaldi" and to the calumnies of the moderates against the just Bertani, but never talk of the ferocious criticisms leveled by Garibaldi himself and many of his advisers against Cavour and the moderates, against the "muddy spirits," the ministerial "lackeys," and the "servants of Napoleon III." Jessie White Mario, however, goes so far as to say that Cavour's death was "a real national calamity, since he alone in Europe was able to face up to the Emperor of the French and cause his plans to fail, and because he already wanted Italy to be one and

strong, and because he did not let his hand be swayed by incompetents. . . ." This is a truly significant *post mortem* eulogy, considering the source from which it comes. We should have expected from Mack Smith more serene recognition of the strong political qualities of the *living* Cavour.

Whenever one speaks of the [rivalry] between Cavour and Garibaldi in the autumn of 1860 or in the winter and spring of 1861, one must keep in mind the pressure of conservative and liberal-conservative Europe upon Italy through the enormous weight of foreign threats, which became more apparent at certain stormy moments—as when the Warsaw Congress met at the end of October 1860 —but were never resolved. In a critical situation such as that in which Cavour had to operate between 1860 and 1861, it was certainly impossible to face up to many problems, to promote a program with constructive goals, or to establish stable and harmonious institutions. Although on the theoretical level democrats might well regret the unachieved ideal of assemblies and of one great national Constituent Assembly, they could not on the level of immediate action envisage anything except an impossible *levée en masse*[6] against a hostile Europe —in short, a kind of laic crusade, still marked by the imprint of Mazzinian mysticism and often displaying some signs of nationalistic lack of balance. By following attentively the development of the arguments, debates, and shifts in opinion, one may study with greater care these less well known aspects of the conflict between the two programs of national policy.

[6] Mobilization of the masses.—*Ed.*

A basic political question in 1860 was whether the formal annexation of central and southern Italy should be effected by means of elected constituent assemblies (which might bargain with Piedmont for a decentralized, federal structure) or by means of a simple plebiscite in which the populace would vote "yes" or "no" to annexation under the existing constitutional structure of Piedmont? GEORGE MACAULAY TREVELYAN (1876–1962) points out that a plebiscitary solution could be accomplished faster in the midst of a delicate international situation.*

Regrettable but Necessary

Cavour . . . as early as October 4 [1860] had gained his point that Garibaldi should invite King [Victor Emmanuel II] and go out to meet him [near Naples]. But for another ten days there was trouble on the further question of the plebiscite, a controversy which became the storm-centre of the last political crisis of the Dictatorship. The question at issue was the proper method of obtaining the consent of the inhabitants of the Neapolitan Kingdom to their absorption in the Monarchy of Victor Emmanuel. Should they be consulted directly by plebiscite, by a simple referendum on the question of annexation, to which each elector could answer by his vote, 'yes' or 'no'? Or should they place their fate in the hands of an assembly of elected representatives, who might then propose conditions on which the South would come into the National union? Such were the two alternatives, and the choice between them was a question of more than mere form.

If Italy had had no armed enemies to fear either within or without the barrier of her guardian Alps, if she had been in safe possession of her own house, then indeed she ought to have gone about the

* From George Macaulay Trevelyan, *Garibaldi and the Making of Italy: June–November, 1860* (London: Longmans, Green & Co., Ltd., 1919), pp. 263–266. Reprinted by permission of Longmans, Green & Co., Ltd.

difficult business of setting it in order with long and careful deliberation. If the union of North and South Italy, like the union of North and South Britain in 1707, had been proposed in a year when the two Kingdoms were immune from invasion and revolution, then indeed a Parliament at Naples and a Parliament at Palermo might reasonably have sat for many months bargaining with the Parliament at Turin. In such a case some of the evils that have actually resulted from a too close union might possibly have been avoided. Those who know South Italy of to-day deplore the rigid and mechanical application of the Piedmontese laws and administrative system to a state of society very different from that of the sub-Alpine populations; and they deplore no less the immense powers of self-government which under the constitution of 1860 have been committed to the backward communes of the South. But this was the necessary price that Italy paid for her existence. In the crisis of that autumn, with war and revolution still in the bowels of the land, with an Austrian army eagerly awaiting the word to cross the Mincio and rush on Milan, with the French Minister already withdrawn from Turin, and every great European Power except England hostile to the unification of Italy, it would have been the height of unwisdom to waste two months in electing and calling together Neapolitan and Sicilian assemblies, and half a year more in bargainings and intrigues of every kind, public and personal, into which Southern Parliamentarians would instinctively plunge and revel, if they found that they had their country in their gift and Cavour on his knees to them to hand it over. If Italian unity were to be accomplished

at all—and all were agreed that there was no other port of safety in sight—then it must be done at once by direct acceptance of Piedmontese law and custom for the whole Peninsula, not because that was best for all but because that alone could be established everywhere without delay. A plebiscite for unconditional annexation could be held in a fortnight, but an assembly might sit until it was dispersed by Austrian bayonets.

The men who in the second week of October besieged Garibaldi with petitions for an assembly instead of the plebiscite, were not, with the exception of the 'federalist' Cattaneo, primarily interested in obtaining a separate system of administration for the South. Their opposition to the plebiscite was essentially factious. Crispi and his friends desired an assembly where they might hope to dominate, and they objected to a plebiscite because it would in a fortnight's time bring to an end the Garibaldian Dictatorship which, so long as it lasted, left the executive power in their hands and kept out the hated Cavour. They played on the Dictator's distrust of the Minister. They cunningly reminded him that the plebiscite had been the device by which Napoleon III had filched Nice and Savoy. There had arisen one of those complicated situations through which Garibaldi was least able to see his way in the light of the few simple rules by which he guided his conduct. His mind was darkened and he sat stupefied at the head of the council-board while the rival parties of plebiscite and assembly defied each other shrilly across the room.

Between October 11 and 13 a series of such councils were held at Caserta and in Naples. Old Giorgio Pallavicino, 'the martyr of the Spielberg,' the Austrian dungeon where he had sat for fourteen years in the early days of the *risorgimento* movement, was now Garibaldi's Pro-Dictator of the Neapolitan mainland. He it was who stood in the breach against Crispi and Cattaneo, on behalf of immediate Italian unity. On October 11, at Caserta, Garibaldi decided for Crispi and an assembly. Pallavicino at once gave in his resignation, and the city of Naples rose in a great demonstration of protest in his favour. On all doors, windows, carriages, coats, and hats appeared cards inscribed *sì* ('yes')—the vote that all desired to be allowed to give in plebiscite. Garibaldi returned to the Capital to find the streets in an uproar. He heard Pallavicino's name coupled with his own for *vivas,* while *morte* was cried out against Mazzini, Crispi, and the others who had persuaded him to summon an assembly. All along the Toledo it 'snowed *sìs*' into the carriage. Garibaldi was much perturbed by this clear manifestation of the popular will, for obedience to the people was one of the formulae of his creed, in accordance with which he had long ago abandoned his republicanism in order to be in touch with his fellow-citizens.

On the thirteenth another council was held in his rooms at the Palazzo d'Angri. Pallavicino refused to take back his resignation unless the plan for an assembly were cancelled. In the middle of an angry dispute between the Pro-Dictator and Crispi, Türr produced a petition signed by thousands of hands in favour of the plebiscite. Garibaldi bowed his head over it in melancholy silence, and for some minutes his face was hidden. When he looked up the clouds had cleared away,

and he wore the 'serene gaiety' of his happiest and gentlest mood. 'If this is the desire of the Neapolitan people,' he said, 'it must be satisfied.' *'Caro Giorgio,'* he said to Pallavicino, 'we need you here still.' The same evening Crispi resigned the secretariate, and his part in the history of Italy came to an end for that year.

The plebiscite was held on October 21. The electorate had no choice but to vote *yes* or *no* to the following proposition: 'The people wishes for Italy one and indivisible with Victor Emmanuel as Constitutional King, and his legitimate descendants after him.' The result was shortly afterwards declared as follows:—

Neapolitan
mainland 1,302,064 yes; 10,312 no
Sicily   432,053 yes;   667 no[1]

The voting was open, and every one who voted 'no' did so in the face of a disapproving world. No doubt, therefore, the real minority was a very much larger proportion of the citizens. But if the plebiscite exaggerated, it did not belie the opinion of the people. Whether the majority of the inhabitants of South Italy wished for Italian unity on its own merits is fairly open to question, but they had shown in more ways than one their earnest desire for immediate and unconditional annexation as the only security against the return of the House of Bourbon and the dreadful past from which Garibaldi had delivered them.

[1] In the Papal dominions the vote, held a few days later, went as follows:—
Marches 133,072 yes; 1,212 no.
Umbria 99,628 yes;   380 no.

The debate over the use of plebiscites rather than constituent assemblies forms a major theme in DENIS MACK SMITH's important study, *Cavour and Garibaldi, 1860: A Study in Political Conflict*. In this passage he cites more or less approvingly an assertion by one of Garibaldi's English confidantes, Jessie White Mario: "To the violent, hurried annexation of the southern provinces was due all the series of disorders and the unhappiness which ensued." In other words, the plebiscites impinged directly on the emergence of Italy's difficult Southern Question. But may not other considerations have contributed to this problem? Does Mack Smith agree with Trevelyan that the international situation necessitated the plebiscites?*

▶ ║║║ *Advanced the Southern Question*

The year 1860 was the *annus mirabilis* [wonderful year] of the Italian *risorgimento*. In the space of a few months, Piedmont-Sardinia more than doubled its size, and combined most of central and all of southern Italy. The formerly independent states of Tuscany, Modena and Parma, with the Papal provinces of the Romagna, Umbria and the Marches, and the far larger area covered by the Two Sicilies, all these invoked the sovereignty of the House of Savoy; and early in 1861 the existence of a new kingdom of Italy was officially proclaimed. Few people were more surprised at the success and speed of this achievement than Cavour, its chief architect; and few more disappointed than Mazzini and Garibaldi, the two men who had looked forward to this moment most keenly and who had sacrificed most for its attainment. Here is a paradox which will serve to indicate at the outset that this was a complicated and controversial passage of history.

The complications and controversies are worth examining for their own sake. They are also important for their influence on the type of state Italy became after 1861, and for the fact that they make a small but interesting chapter in

* From Denis Mack Smith, *Cavour and Garibaldi, 1860: A Study in Political Conflict* (Cambridge, England: University Press, 1954), pp. 1, 4–6, 442–444, omitting the original footnotes. Reprinted by permission of Cambridge University Press.

the larger history of nationalism. The subject is more accurately studied in particular than in general. . . .

Very briefly, the central theme is as follows. In April 1860 a revolt broke out among Sicilians against the Bourbon government at Naples. This was in the main a local movement against administrative oppression; but incidentally it became tinged with politics, for it had been actively encouraged by the radicals, and was accepted only with some reluctance by the moderate liberals. Then in May the arrival of Garibaldi with his Thousand from the north confirmed and continued this radical inspiration of the revolt. The name of Garibaldi was a guarantee that the battle would be fought for Italy and not just for the local needs of Sicily, but it also represented political ideals very different from those of Cavour. Garibaldi was a great soldier, and the revolution developed with unexpected success beneath his protection and encouragement. In July he marched through to the eastern seaboard of Sicily. In August he crossed over to Calabria. On 7 September he entered Naples, and soon the whole of southern Italy up to the River Volturno was under his radical dictatorship. Later in September he felt strong enough to begin his march on Rome, and even to ask that Cavour be dismissed from the post of prime minister. But then, suddenly, the political direction of the movement changed, and Garibaldi was manoeuvred into a position where he had to surrender. Cavour's troops invaded Naples before the revolt could spread to Rome. On 21 October, Sicily and Naples elected by plebiscite for the merger of all the south into the kingdom governed from Turin by Victor Emanuel. This vote brought the revolution to a close. It represented a notable victory for Cavour, who had dramatically captured the political and military initiative.

As a result the radicals had to wait many years for the partial attainment of their various desires: until 1870 for the realization of Garibaldi's designs on Rome; until 1876 for the victory of Depretis and the Left in parliament; until the turn of the century for recognition of the special economic and social needs of the south; and until after 1946 for the achievement of Mazzini's republican dream and Cattaneo's cherished ideal of regional autonomy. And yet a false picture will be given if it is assumed in advance that, in the year 1860, a monarchic and unitary state was the only conclusion which had any chance of emerging from the revolution. For in fact, although the method of a plebiscite seemed to lead easily enough to the creation of a united kingdom, many people had feared until the last moment that a constituent assembly might meet instead, and that a federalist or a republican solution would be considered.

This alternative of plebiscite or constituent assembly became the issue round which the various political programmes took shape in southern Italy. The victory of the plebiscite marked the success of one set of ideas and one set of men over another. The limitations and incompleteness of this victory, as well as the manner of its achievement, were to be of great importance for the future history of Italy. Not only did they bear directly on the emergence of a 'southern question' in Italian politics, but neither the radicals nor the regionalists were ever quite reconciled to finding the fruit of their labours plucked by other people. The tensions set up between the various regions and political parties were never to be properly resolved. Some of the ablest of Italian politicians were kept for decades in unproductive opposition, and, when at last they were accepted into the ruling élite, were too old to learn the delicate art of responsible government. The southern provinces were also taught by this victory and its aftermath to resent the domination of the 'Piedmontese' —as their new governors from the north were generically termed. Political opposition thus became identified in part with regional opposition, and this in turn with social and religious opposition; for little effort was made to reconcile either the southern peasants or the Church to this sudden triumph of a secular, middle-class state.

Cavour has his place secure among the greatest statesmen and the greatest liberals of any nation. Few historical characters have had such a consistently 'good press' since their death. And yet, as with all historical figures, his true stature will be understood only if he is looked at with a critical eye. Wherever historians can spend longer studying a statesman's reaction to a problem than that statesman once spent on the problem itself, it often occurs that events appear to have happened more unpredictably and with less conscious purpose behind them than had formerly been thought. It also becomes possible to question some of the legends left behind by historical recollection. It will be seen that Cavour was by no means infallible; and his chosen colleagues often fell far short of what the moment required. The kingdom of Italy, which they did so much to create, was one of the most notable achievements of the age, and this gives to these critical

months of its formation a particular interest. Nevertheless, in some important respects it was to prove highly unstable; and many Italians agreed that this was due to flaws in its original creation. . . .

The plebiscites in the south rounded off the process by which a kingdom of four or five millions in population became one of twenty-two millions. The radical Crispi could fairly claim that 'what you call our "faction" has shed its blood for the cause of national unity and presented half Italy to the house of Savoy.' Crispi himself had a great future to look forward to in the new kingdom of Italy; but Garibaldi and Mazzini now found that their work was mostly done. Garibaldi returned to his bees and his beans on the island of Caprera, Mazzini sadly went back into exile at London. In February 1861 Mazzini wrote a memorandum in English for the British foreign minister, protesting against Cavour's 'rancour against all other parties and men, and innate antagonism to popular interference and all that he calls *revolutionary*.' It was bitter for this visionary to see that materialism had succeeded to idealism. He had thought to evoke the soul of Italy, he said, but all he now found before him was its corpse. And yet Mazzini's faith in the future remained as clear and confident as ever. 'Our nationality is not a thing merely of square miles but of ideas and principles. And as soon as Italy will learn that she may proceed in her work with the whole of her forces and shielded from Bonapartist interference, she will desert the policy of Cavour for a better and more dignified one.' This was the faith which, in one very real sense, removed mountains. The combination of square miles and idealistic principles together made up a force which was unbeatable.

Meanwhile, the only consolation left to the radicals was perhaps to say 'I told you so.' Long after the event, Jessie White Mario, who had been one of Garibaldi's entourage in Sicily and Naples, wrote that

to the violent, hurried annexation of the southern provinces was due all the series of disorders and the unhappiness which ensued.

If only these provinces had been administered sensibly and kindly by persons sympathetic to the people, as Tuscany was for example, there would have been none of that boycotting of conscription in Sicily, nor the brigandage which raged in the Napoletano.

This was only part of the truth, but it was an important part; and the storm of recrimination between moderates and extremists on this point was to remain a constant theme of Italian politics.

In this selection, which comes from L. C. B. SEAMAN's provocative interpretation of nineteenth-century European history, the author argues that neither central nor southern Italy was ready for unification, and that Garibaldi was to blame for pushing the pace of unification. Furthermore, the plebiscites in favor of annexation to the House of Savoy proved only certain negative propositions. What were these propositions? Does Seaman share the opinion attributed to Jessie White Mario in the preceding selection that the plebiscites were partly to blame for the emergence of Italy's Southern Question?*

▶ ‖ *Proved Only Negative Propositions*

Contrary to Cavour's expectations and hopes, Garibaldi succeeded in Sicily. Cavour's aim at once was to get Sicily annexed to Piedmont. Garibaldi wanted annexation too, but not before he had reached Rome. He calculated that once Sicily passed into Piedmontese control he would be unable to use it as he intended to use it, namely as the supply base for his attack on Naples and Rome. This was precisely why Cavour wanted Sicily annexed forthwith, and why Garibaldi would not agree. Another reason for delay imposed itself. Sicilians wanted to be free of the Bourbons and of Naples, but hardly any of them wanted annexation to Piedmont. Incorporation into a Kingdom of all Italy they might agree to: but that would be possible only when such a kingdom existed—after and not before Garibaldi had proclaimed it from Rome, its true capital. Another complication was that Cavour could not simply grab Sicily. It was the property of the Bourbon government in Naples; and as a diplomat Cavour realized he had to be careful. The English, true, had no objections; but Napoleon III demanded a plebiscite, so that there could be a public appeal from the law of nations to the

* From L. C. B. Seaman, *From Vienna to Versailles* (New York: Coward-McCann, Inc., 1956), pp. 81-82, 86-91. Copyright 1956 by Coward-McCann, Inc. Reprinted by permission of Coward-McCann, Inc., New York, and Methuen & Co. Ltd., London.

higher principle of nationality. Yet, since hardly anybody in Sicily could read, hardly anybody wanted annexation to Piedmont, and nobody would do anything against the wishes of Garibaldi (who was already at the gates of Naples and might soon be in Rome) an early plebiscite was impossible. In an atmosphere of confusion and rather unnecessary ill-will, Cavour worked from the remote distance of Turin to get control of a situation for which he was entirely unprepared. . . .

The plain fact was that in 1860 Italy was not ready for unification under Piedmont, and Piedmont was neither ready nor fitted for the responsibilities of governing a unified Italy. If Cavour and the Piedmontese must bear a large proportion of the blame for the disappointments that mark the early history of the Italian kingdom, Garibaldi has his responsibilities in the matter also. The revolutionary attempt to steal a march on history, to force the pace of human change in the interests of passionately held beliefs and theories, is always a mistake. The human mind is capable of just so much change and no more: it can never willingly move as fast as idealists want it to. Under the impulse of extravagant hopes and mass enthusiasm men can move very fast at revolutionary epochs; but the hopes and the enthusiasm are so much spiritual benzedrine and speedily produce a contrary reaction. The aftermath is mental disillusionment and social disarray. Garibaldi forced the pace in 1860; but it was a pace that all but killed the spirit of the Risorgimento in Italy.

The centre and south were not ready for unification, and the plebiscites in favour of annexation to the house of Savoy proved only certain negative propositions. The enormous number of voters who said 'yes' to annexation by Piedmont said so because to vote against it was, in the circumstances of 1860, a vote without meaning, a vote for the impossible. It could imply nothing more than a wish to continue the prevailing confusion of an interregnum that could easily develop into anarchy and civil war. All the plebiscites really proved was that people were tired of the uncertainty that had prevailed since Garibaldi's first landing in Sicily, and therefore preferred annexation as the only visible means of getting settled government again. As to the sort of settled government they would prefer, the plebiscites gave them no chance to express an opinion about that. What is more, Cavour was determined at all costs that no chance to express an opinion should be permitted. Consequently the votes in the plebiscites represented not a rational decision in favour of anything, but a sort of emotional *te deum* proclaiming a general sense of thankfulness that the time of troubles was at an end.

Unhappily the troubles were not at an end. The real troubles of southern Italy and Sicily were not political but social and economic. Poverty, illiteracy and a great shortage of land; these were the essential facts of the situation. And since the Bourbons had not invented these facts, the departure of the Bourbons did not alter them. Worse still, the assimilation of the south to the Piedmontese system did not merely fail to settle the fundamental problems of the south; it made them worse. The most obvious immediate consequences of the Risorgimento in the south, and the creation of a Kingdom of all Italy, were conscription, higher taxation, an increased cost of living, and a brand new legal system centred upon Turin. Within a matter of weeks after the plebiscites, great tides of opinion in the south had turned against Victor Emmanuel and Piedmont; and the outstanding feature of southern Italy after 1860 was uncontrollable and widespread brigandage, combining the characteristics of a peasants' revolt and a Bourbon counter-revolution. Only if words are used in the narrowest and most legalistic sense is it permissible to say that Italy was united in 1860; for the new régime was rejected spiritually and politically by the more pious Catholics, and rejected physically to the point of open warfare by the southern peasants.

These perhaps inevitable consequences of the rapid annexation of the south by Piedmont were due to the fact that Garibaldi had forced the hand of the Piedmontese too. Cavour knew nothing of the south of Italy and did not even dare to show his face in liberated Naples. He and his agents were quite unfitted to the task of governing the south with sympathy or even intelligence. It was all very well for Garibaldi to hand his territories over to the re galantuomo and then go off to Caprera; but it was Cavour and his successors who were to have to manage these territories. Garibaldi had the satisfaction of doing his duty; Victor Emmanuel had the satisfaction of being the first king of all Italy. But it was Cavour who was left holding the baby; and if he and his successors did the job badly at least they have the excuse that it was Garibaldi's baby, not theirs.

Various expressions used by leading figures in Piedmont in 1860 indicate the state of mind in which the Piedmontese approached the problem of governing the south. The Neapolitans were 'canaille'; they were 'barbarians who cared little for liberty'; Naples was 'rotten to the marrow,' it was an Augean stable, and it was 'not Italy, but Africa.' And the Piedmontese knew so little of economic realities that they were convinced that there was great wealth in the south and that all that was wrong was the shiftless character of the Neapolitans. For the great weakness of Cavour's Liberalism, like most Liberalism (and theoretical Socialism also), was that it was cursed with an urban parochialism of mind. It neither understood nor cared for the problems of backward, rural societies: its entire philosophy reflected the needs of ambitious metropolitan man, whether he was a would-be industrialist, an aspiring member of the professional classes, or a progressively minded aristocrat who saw in an attack on the old feudal and ecclesiastical system more opportunity for the increase of his own wealth and power than he could get by defending that system. Free institutions, free trade, unrestricted opportunities for the commercial, industrial and professional middle class —these were the aims of Cavour and his allies, and these alone. Moreover, they were aims which were put in jeopardy by Garibaldi's policy of war and still more war, of revolution through the common people. Rigidly and rightly proud of their superior efficiency, pharisaically conscious of being in the van of progress, the Piedmontese Liberals were contemptuous of the people of the south for their ignorance, hostile to their religious feelings, and convinced that their low standard of living was due to their incorrigible idleness rather than to the intractability of nature. Granted that only the Piedmontese possessed adequate administrative training, and therefore had to govern the South because there were few indigenous administrators of experience, it is still unfortunate that Piedmont treated the people of the south with the arrogance of conquerors imposing alien institutions on a tribe of barbarians for their own good.

In this second passage from his perceptive study on the thought and action of the *Risorgimento,* LUIGI SALVATORELLI discusses the attitudes of Garibaldi and Mazzini toward the plebiscitary method of annexation of the south. Were these two men dogmatic in their opposition to plebiscites? What do you think of Salvatorelli's point that the Mazzinian foes of plebiscitary unification failed to appreciate the possibility that a liberal regime of Cavour's type might later initiate significant political and social reforms?*

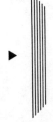 *Did Not Prevent Future Reforms*

In the contest between Mazzini and Cavour, as well as in the contest over the question of whether to proceed by means of a constituent assembly (which would complete the popular initiative) or by means of a plebiscite (which would give democratic consecration to the royal initiative), Garibaldi tipped the scales in favor of Cavour. This was true even though Garibaldi proclaimed himself a republican and opposed Cavour only slightly less than did Mazzini. In his famous toast in London in 1864, Garibaldi proclaimed Mazzini to be his teacher. Later, after the dispute with him and

more especially with the Mazzinians became poisoned and cancerous, Garibaldi sought to deny this, asserting that he had been an Italian and a republican from infancy without owing anything to Mazzini.

Actually, Mazzini was Garibaldi's teacher, as he was of many others, but the spiritual make-up of the disciple was, and continued to be, quite different from his own. Garibaldi was the ideal leader of a popular war, the *condottiere* capable of leading and commanding individual citizens on the battlefield, of inflaming them and enlisting them in support of

* From Luigi Salvatorelli, *Pensiero e azione del Risorgimento,* 6th edition (Turin: Giulio Einaudi Editore, 1960), pp. 157-158, 165-168, translated by Charles F. Delzell. Reprinted by permission of Giulio Einaudi Editore.

the national cause, with a native personal disinterest that was ingenuously heroic. He was the incarnation of the Italian national and popular spirit that longed for independence, freedom, and justice in all its primitive force, in all its immediate purity. He was much closer to the people than was Mazzini; he understood them and was understood by them much better. But precisely because he embodied so well the popular conscience in all its ingenuousness, he was incapable of rising above it, of guiding it toward distant and ultimate goals. The second part of the Mazzinian diptych, "thought and action," he executed marvelously and much better than the first part. A man of much more realistic temperament than Mazzini, he was also much shallower in thought and less farsighted in vision. The Mazzinian conception of popular "self-creation" escaped him, and the ultimate religious foundation of the Mazzinian program remained alien to him.

Although he sincerely believed in the abstract superiority of the republic, Garibaldi halted when he perceived, with common sense, that it was impossible to proclaim an Italian republic in 1860. And since at the same time he broadened his conception of a republic to include within it any kind of government that was approved by the people (if the English were happy with Queen Victoria's government, he said, then this must be regarded as being republican), he decided with no misgivings that the plebiscites had consecrated Victor Emmanuel's monarchy, and thereafter he quit worrying about the details of this problem.

Nor did he worry over the additional political issue involved in Mazzini's request for a constituent assembly. To him this seemed simply a waste of time. As soon as he recognized that he could not proceed from Naples to Rome and to Venice, Garibaldi no longer had any reason to delay the annexations. As far as he was concerned, the political ramifications of the problem disappeared behind its territorial aspects. His attitude toward the problem reflected his conviction that in order to achieve Italian national unification (as well as unifications of other countries), one must make temporary use of dictatorship, in this instance of Victor Emmanuel's dictatorship. He did not take into consideration that this was not a case of "temporary" dictatorship, but rather of establishing a dynasty permanently. Only much later, after 1870, did Garibaldi speak out like Mazzini regarding the inadequacy of the Sardinian constitution and of the need for replacing it with a national pact.

Mazzini intended that the Italian people, acting freely, directly, and integrally as a national community, should decide for themselves the kind of political regime they wished. He advocated "a national pact," to be drawn up by a constituent assembly. Even [Vincenzo] Gioberti had written [in 1851] in his *Rinnovamento* [d'Italia] that after the Piedmontese dictatorship and as a necessary aspect of the liberation and formation of Italy, an all-inclusive national assembly must be convened to establish the political and juridical foundation of the nation. For Mazzini, plebiscites were not the equivalent of a constituent assembly and a pact produced by it. This was true because the plebiscites were not preceded by discussions in an arena of free political interplay; because the plebiscite formulas allowed for no alternative other than union with the constitutional kingdom of Victor Emmanuel II; and because the plebiscites implied blind acceptance by all of Italy of a constitution that was strictly Piedmontese in nature and bestowed by royal concession.

He saw this [type of unification] not as a truly popular creation of a new Italy, but as working itself out simply by means of external aggregation, almost as a conquest. And there could not but be confirmation of this interpretation when Parliament in its vote to establish the Kingdom of Italy (and it was a parliament that had been elected by a very narrow franchise) proclaimed Victor Emmanuel as the Second and not the First. To Mazzini's way of thinking, as well as that of republican federalists and most democrats, this signified the continuation of the House of Savoy and not the creation of a new Italian monarchy. This signified divine right, not popular right —divine right which, even though coupled with the phrase "will of the nation" (though this was also included for the purpose of excluding the papal theocracy), openly displayed itself in the official titles of acts by the new kingdom.

This judgment by Mazzini cannot be regarded (as "moderate liberals" used to and still contend) simply as a dogmatic apriority or even as a sectarian deformity. One should distinguish between Mazzini's judgment as to the way in which the political and juridical structure was established during unification in 1860-1861 and his other judgment regarding the future possibilities and types of political behavior inherent in an Italian state so constituted. As to the first point, the verdict of history has come to agree substantially with the Mazzinian judgment (and also with the federal republican one). The fact needs to be emphasized (although everyone can evaluate it as he pleases. . .) that the process whereby the Kingdom of Italy was formed— namely, annexations by means of plebiscites and Parliament—did not involve a constitution drawn up by the Italian people on the basis of enlightened reflection and freedom of action. Instead, unification was achieved by improvisation based on necessity, and it represented a compromise between popular forces and conservative dynastic power. It was achieved under the three-fold pressure of the only Italian state still on its feet; of European diplomacy; and of the absence, at least in immediate prospects, of any other acceptable solution that would not be a return to the previous state of affairs, or to foreign occupation, or to anarchy. Everyone—from Victor Emmanuel and Cavour to Garibaldi and Mazzini—acted on this basis and adopted the principle, "What's done is done," which Gioberti had taught in his *Rinnovamento*. This improvisation based on necessity translated itself into the imperfect character of the plebiscites and into the ratification of these by a Parliament elected by restricted suffrage, and in the pure and simple adoption of the very same constitution that Charles Albert had bestowed upon Piedmont in 1848 in circumstances that had aroused Mazzinian opposition. This improvisation . . . was not . . . in its immediate political and juridical reality a truly genuine creation of the new nation-state. Instead it was the absorption of all the other Italian states by one of the previously existing ones.

Mazzini's dogmatic and static mentality deduced from these correct observations a definitely negative judgment and an absolutely stubborn prejudice against the new state. Thus he reverted with respect to the Kingdom of Italy to the position of revolutionary intransigence that he had maintained toward the old Italian states. Because of his characteristic lack of a certain liberal mentality, he did not see how, in view of all the past bunglings, the improvised new state could possess any substantial newness or possibility of cleansing itself of its original sin. Yet the real novelty of the situation was this liberal regime. Stronger than Achilles' lance, it could heal the wounds of others as well as its own. In the course of day-to-day political battles it could test, modify, and transform this creation in the most radical fashion. In the course of day-to-day political battles it could validate, if it wished, what had been improvised out of necessity at the moment of unification.

The truth is that it was not only Mazzini who displayed a dogmatic and static mentality with respect to the Kingdom of Italy. This mentality was even more pronounced among his moderately liberal foes and even among those in the Action Party who swung their support to the new Kingdom, for they came to regard the plebiscites as an untouchable fetish rather than as a first step in a continuous political process. They regarded the parliamentary oath as the juridical consecration of this untouchability, and in this way they deformed and falsified the conception of national sovereignty and initi-

ative that was the true basis of the *Risorgimento.*

A major consequence of this "construction out of necessity" (that is, the establishment of the Kingdom of Italy through the parliamentary and annexationist process which we have described) was that the common people, because they had not participated directly in the construction [of the state], could not even make it take cognizance of their interests. Thus the social program of the *Risorgimento* that had been set forth by Mazzini, by [Giuseppe] Ferrari,[1] by Gioberti in the *Rinnovamento,* and most boldly of all by [Carlo] Pisacane[2] (whereas the moderates and even Cavour had largely ignored it) was left on the sidelines by the new state. This was the negative social side of "moderatism," of that compromising tendency that permeated the formation of the Kingdom of Italy—an aspect that was complementary to the political side of the process, or was rather . . . its necessary consequence, inasmuch as the principle, *politique d'abord* [politics come first], is always true. Nevertheless, for this particular deficiency, just as for the broader ones, the possibility of remedial action existed within the liberal regime.

[1] A Milanese political philosopher (1811–1876) who advocated a federalist system of Italian unification.—*Ed.*

[2] A democratic nationalist and precursor of the socialist movement in Italy (1818–1857) who lost his life in an abortive invasion of the Kingdom of the Two Sicilies.—*Ed.*

Unification of Italy took place partly at the expense of the territory of the Papal States. Moreover, most Italian nationalists dreamed of the day when Rome would become the capital of the unified state. In the last months of his life Premier Cavour devised the formula, "A free church in a free state," in the hope of circumventing the papal doctrine of the "temporal power" (that is, the theory that the pope must hold sovereignty over territory in order to fulfill his spiritual mission). What exactly did Cavour's formula imply? Negotiations between Turin and Rome got under way in 1861 and then collapsed. Why? WILLIAM ROSCOE THAYER, the New England Protestant biographer of Cavour already quoted, argues here that the Jesuits surrounding Pope Pius IX (1846–1878) were to blame. Is his evidence convincing?*

Pius IX and the Jesuits Responsible

[For the completion of Italian unification after 1860] one thing was absolutely essential—Rome. When North, Centre and South were welded together, Rome alone could satisfy the conflicting requirements of a capital. To Neapolitans and Sicilians, Turin seemed a foreign city. Lombards insisted that Milan should be preferred to it. Tuscans clung to Florence. On the other hand, the Piedmontese pleaded with justifiable devotion that Turin, the cradle of national independence, the asylum of Italian patriots, the residence of the King, the home of the Subalpine Parliament, should continue to be the capital. Without Rome, geography pointed to Florence, as being nearest to the Centre: but considerations of geography cannot smooth away prejudices or even compensate for civic emotions and patriotic desires. Cavour wished that there might be two capitals—his beloved Turin for business, and Rome for state and pleasure: but he knew that personal preference ought not to weigh against the supreme national considerations. Rome was neutral—Milanese or Florentines, Turinese or Neapolitans could not set up their local city before her. Rome was uni-

* From William Roscoe Thayer, *The Life and Times of Cavour* (Boston and New York: Houghton Mifflin Company, 1911), vol. II, pp. 442-452, omitting the original footnotes. Reprinted by permission of Houghton Mifflin Company.

versal, the symbol of unity for Italians, the centre to which, from the remotest corners of the world, all roads led. Ricasoli not less than Garibaldi acknowledged the spell of Rome. Mazzini had long prophesied the Third Rome, which should be to modern life what Imperial Rome was to antiquity and Papal Rome to the Middle Age.

Sentiment, political expediency, history, the claims of structural symmetry and of geographical convenience, called for Rome as the capital of Italy. But Rome was the seat of the Roman Catholic Pope, who happened also to be a petty Italian despot.

The Papacy, the temporal institution, stricken with senility, infected with the vices of old age when it is corrupt, had for sixty years required foreign support to save it from its own subjects. Now, however, Austria, the pledged protectress of despotism in Italy, had been expelled; a large part of the Papal territory had already been united to the new Kingdom; and if the French garrison were withdrawn, the narrow Patrimony of St. Peter would throw over Papal government in a day. The time seemed propitious, therefore, for persuading the Pope to come to terms with modern conditions. He could hope nothing more from Austria; the Catholic Powers had not lifted a finger to prevent the spoliation of the Legations; the French Emperor was known to be tired of propping up the ungrateful and incompetent Papal régime; Pius could be satisfied that he had loyally striven to preserve intact the impossible political legacy handed down from one pope to another since the Renaissance.

Cavour's splendid project, however, did not stop short at securing the predes-tined capital for United Italy; it went on to embrace the vision of a renewed Church, whose influence would be immeasurably enhanced as soon as it was freed from its worldly consort. Impressed by the part which religion should play in the life of a people, he recognized, as many of the devoutest Catholics of that century recognized, that one of the chief causes of moral decadence and spiritual torpor was the confusing of religion and politics. So he aimed at a solution in which, by the divorce of Church and State, the service of God should no longer be neglected for the service of Mammon. As a proof that this was his desire, he based his first appeal to the Pontiff on the benefits which religion would derive from the proposed compact. Free from hatred and malice, he approached the question with the detachment of a mathematician, who endeavors to discover a solution which shall be approved long after the original parties to the transaction have vanished. This habit of his of subordinating his personal feelings for the sake of the cause —as he had done in his relations with Garibaldi—was so unusual, that his critics failed to recognize it, or if they faintly surmised it, they imputed it to hypocrisy.

In order to make Rome the capital of United Italy, he must either persuade the Pope to consent to give up his temporal power, or, if that failed, arrange with Napoleon to withdraw the French garrison, upon which the Eternal City would speedily welcome the Italians. He proposed to exhaust his efforts with Rome direct, before trying the roundabout and less satisfactory dealings with Paris. After the occupation of Umbria and the Marches, Cavour asked Diomede Pantaleoni, a physician at Rome, who was a friend both of Cavour and of several of the cardinals, to sound very discreetly whether there were any possibility of opening the way to a reconciliation. In the course of a fortnight, Pantaleoni sent a favorable reply; and he made such progress that by the middle of December [1860] he presented a memorial to one of the most influential cardinals. This was Santucci, known as the opponent of that Antonellian policy by which the Papacy had been wrecked and the Church was being forced back into medieval intransigence. Pantaleoni's rough draft of proposals began with Cavour's formula, "A Free Church in a Free State," and specified that the Pope should relinquish temporal power, in return for which he should be acknowledged as nominal sovereign, inviolable in his person, absolutely free to exercise his ecclesiastical functions according to canonical forms, to communicate with the clergy in Italy and abroad, and to convoke synods. He should retain the Vatican and certain other palaces, besides receiving a munificent annual subsidy. To the clergy should be assigned revenues sufficient to support every priest who had the cure of souls entrusted to him. Liberty of teaching and of preaching, of founding theological schools and ecclesiastical corporations, was stipulated, subject only to the civil laws which applied to all persons in the Kingdom.

Before these bare proposals were made, however, Cavour wished to prepare the minds of the Papalists by showing the benefits which the compact would bring to the Church. The Italian people, he said, was profoundly Catholic. Schism had never taken deep roots among them. All the more desirable, therefore, was it that the antagonism between them and the directors of their religion should cease. Much of that antagonism was traceable to the fact that in his character of Italian prince the Pope had seemed a political rival to his fellow Italian princes, who had consequently imposed many restrictions upon his ecclesiastical functions. Hence the Tannuccian Laws in Naples, the Leopoldine laws in Tuscany, the Josephine Laws in the Austrian provinces; hence concordats, bargains and reciprocal favors with the Catholic Powers outside the Peninsula. "To vindicate the complete independence of the Church from the State in spiritual affairs," he urged, "is doubtless the noblest and loftiest mission that Pope Pius IX could undertake." He pointed out that the failure of the recent concordat with Austria showed that the method chosen to secure it was not the best adapted to either the spirit of the times or the actual aspirations of Christian peoples. Italy, he said, was the only Catholic country which could aid Pius to fulfil his glorious mission, and Victor Emmanuel the only sovereign who could set the example of renouncing franchises, to guard which had been till then one of the hinges of European politics. By these and other considerations, Cavour hoped that the Pope and his advisers would realize that the great boon of a Free Church must far more than offset the loss of Temporal Power. That Temporal Power itself had been hewn down to a precarious minimum, which would vanish in turn whenever the French evacuated Rome. As the Church had always been strongest when the Papacy was weakest, so the culmination of the Papacy, when in its luxury, splendor and worldliness it surpassed the other unbridled princedoms of the Renaissance, saw the falling away from Catholicism of half of Christendom, followed by the degeneration of Italy, Spain and Portugal and the spread of scepticism in France. Providence seemed to have set before the Pope the opportunity of making the Church once more a mighty religious and moral influence, untrammeled by the political, mundane and corrupting interests of the Papacy.

Cavour hoped that, though his appeal to the spiritual side should fail, the practical benefits which he offered would win over the Pope and his counsellors. He believed that, when the bishops and lower clergy understood what the change would mean to them, they would welcome it. To the objection that he was conceding too much—that the Church, freed from the Papacy, would acquire a real influence over the country—he replied: "I do not fear liberty in any of its applications." He did not allow the fact that the Curia was the most reactionary body in the Roman Catholic world to discourage him.

Although the details of the negotiations have never been officially revealed, we can trace with some definiteness the course taken by Cavour's agents. Pantaleoni was joined by Father Passaglia, a Jesuit, who had commended himself to the Pope by writing a strong polemic in behalf of the dogma of the Immaculate Conception, and who now, being convinced of the immense harm which the moribund Temporal Power was causing the Church, bravely advocated its abolition. Passaglia and Pantaleoni found sympathetic hearers in Cardinals Santucci and D'Andrea, and probably some others, whose names were held back. Their reports cheered Cavour, who regarded any rift in the Cardinals' College as a hopeful sign. He wrote Passaglia on February 21, 1861: "I trust that, before this coming Easter, you will send me an olive branch, symbol of eternal peace between the Church and the State, between the Papacy and the Italians. If that comes to pass, the joy of the Catholic world will be greater than that which, nearly nineteen centuries ago, the entry of our Lord into Jerusalem produced." On January 13, Cavour received a despatch announcing that when Cardinal Santucci spoke out, the Pope appeared to resign himself to the suggested surrender of the Temporal Power; then Antonelli was called, and he too, after a brief opposition, seemed to acquiesce. Both he and Santucci begged the Pope to release them from their oath, in order that they might be canonically free to treat this question. Cavour secretly informed Napoleon III of the transaction and received word that the Emperor hoped he would proceed, although he predicted that there was slight chance of success. Before authorizing even an officious overture, Cavour still waited. Passaglia had an interview with Pius and Antonelli, from which he made favorable deductions, and went to Turin to confer with the Prime Minister, who had taken Minghetti and Artom into the secret. When the Jesuit Father returned to Rome, he bore with him the systematized proposals. During the next two or three weeks, he and Pantaleoni felt their way towards a favorable moment; but the Jesuits already had wind of the intrigue, and they drew so close a ring round Pius that Cardinal d'Andrea advised that Cavour should instruct his agents to go direct to the Pope and tell him that the Government would be glad to negotiate. Cavour consented. His credentials scarcely reached Rome, however, before Pantaleoni was commanded to quit the city within twenty-four hours. What had happened? We can only conjecture as to what induced Antonelli's sudden revulsion—for he it was who gave the drastic order.

While Passaglia and Pantaleoni had been attempting to work upon the Pope through the more Liberal Cardinals, other Cavourian agents—Omero Bozino, Salvator Aguglia, one of Antonelli's intimates, and Antonio Isaia, secretary of the Dataria—approached Antonelli himself. As it was certain that Pius would take no final action without the approval of his political mentor, common sense dictated the expediency of propitiating that personage. Bozino, therefore, drew up general overtures similar in most respects to Pantaleoni's. In addition he proposed that the Italian Government should approve all the contracts made by the Antonelli family with the Papal Government, besides bestowing on Cardinal Antonelli himself three million lire, and conferring special honors upon his brothers. The price would have been cheap, most Italians would have declared, to pay for amputating the Papal cancer from Italy and the Catholic world. Antonelli, whose piety could be reached only through his purse, is described as being ready to close the bargain; for after Castelfidardo he looked upon the Temporal Power as lost and was watching for the best way in which to provide for his own future. According to Isaia and Aguglia the negotiation had gone so far that nothing more was needed except Antonelli's signature to the compact, before he presented it to the consistory. Then without warning, the transaction blew up. Pantaleoni fled from Rome on March 21, and was soon followed by Isaia and Passaglia. What made Antonelli change his mind?

The leaking out of the secret, says Isaia: but the Cardinal needed only to disavow any knowledge of the affair, in order to remain diplomatically correct. More probably he found in the Curia so strong a body of opponents to the scheme, that he deemed it safer to cast it aside, at least for the present. The coming to Rome of the Bourbon King and Queen after the fall of Gaeta must also be taken into account. In collusion with the Pope's Government they were organizing brigandage on a vast scale and labeling it a holy war. The condition of the Kingdom of Italy was so disturbed that Francis and his fellow-pretenders might dream that either civil war or foreign intervention would give them a chance to recover their thrones. So long as that chance existed, the wary Antonelli might very well reason that it would be foolish to throw away the Temporal Power. Pius also, from being resigned, became suddenly immovable. Had his Jesuit entourage intimidated him? Did he remember that Clement XIV, the last pope who had dared to resist the Company of Jesus, sickened mysteriously and died, of poison their enemies believed? On March 18, he uttered an encyclical breathing anathema upon the government at Turin, and that same day, he flew into one of his periodic rages and so berated Santucci that the poor Cardinal lost his mind and died insane a few months later.

Thus ended, not inappropriately in a burst of pontifical fury, Cavour's attempt to harmonize Church and State in Italy. Cynics smiled at seeing him outwitted, as they thought, by Antonelli. The friendly rather pitied him as the victim of a Utopian aberration. Those who knew the circuitous methods of the Curia said that he had not taken time enough. But the underlying obstacle was the astuteness with which the Curia, composed almost wholly of Italians, used the doctrine of the Temporal Power to serve their own ends and to perpetuate the preponderance of the Italians in the hierarchy.

The claim that the Temporal Power was indispensable to the Pope's spiritual functions was, like the claim of the divine right of kings, a comparatively modern invention. In the New Testament there is not a hint that a religious leader must also possess political authority. Herod, not Jesus, was King of Judea. The disciples of Jesus and their successors acquired no pomp as satrap or proconsul. It was only in the Renaissance that the King usurped the first place over the Pope in the Pope-King partnership. Popes not only used the Papacy to build up the fortunes of their families; they even disposed of Papal territory for their private benefits. The cynical remark attributed to the sybarite, Leo the Tenth, that "we Medici have profited mightily by the legend of Jesus Christ," though apocryphal, set forth an evident fact. And as the pontiffs' incapacity to govern what remained of the Kingdom of the Church became notorious, they protested all the more vehemently that their temporal rule was necessary to the Church. Such stubbornness is common to men and institutions far gone in senility. Yet no Papalist would admit that during the exile of Pius VI and VII, when the Papal State ceased to exist for fifteen years, or during the Republican interregnum of 1848–49, the decrees of the Church were diminished by a hair's breadth in authority. The historic evolution of the Papacy was clear to anyone allowed to consult history; but when the politicians of the Curia saw Temporal Power slipping away, they insisted more desperately on its preservation, and some of them would have embodied it in a dogma. The reasons chiefly urged by them were that without the Temporal Power the Pope might be hindered in his communications with the Catholic world, or he might fall under the influence of the Italian Government. To this Liberal Italians replied that as the Pope had depended since 1815 upon the armed protection of either France or Austria, or of both, he could not be regarded as free, while the fact that the sovereigns of Austria, France, Spain and Portugal could and did exercise a veto at the election of a pope, was proof direct of secular interference. Many declared that the true reason for pressing the claim to Temporal Power could not be avowed: it was to prevent the monopoly of the Catholic hierarchy from passing out of the hands of Italians. The offices, the sinecures, above all the power, should not be shared with foreign Catholics; four sevenths of the College of Cardinals and nine tenths of the Papal bureaucracy should remain Italian. Foreign Catholics, at least among the higher ecclesiastics, accepted this condition, because it gave them a special authority at home. The foreign cardinal or bishop owed his place not to his local sovereign but to the Pope; and if there were conflict of interest, he sided with the Pope. In many cases these ecclesiastics connived with pretenders, in the hope of getting larger favors for themselves. Conversely, a Legitimist pretender, in France, for instance, would have no hesitation in making lavish promises to Clerical supporters. Thus while the hierarchy was being exploited for the benefit of the crafty Italian minority, foreign ecclesiastics acquiesced because the arrangement gave them certain privileges in return for their birthright. They were, moreover, scattered in many countries, so that a union among them against the central authority would be difficult, if not impossible. As a result, if any local movement gathered volume enough to send delegates to Rome, those delegates were quickly ground to powder by the great machine, which was always orthodox and always Roman.

Now Cavour appealed from the Pope as a petty temporal sovereign, to the Pope as the head of a world religion—from mundane ambition to conscience. He had in view not merely the immediate benefits that would come to 25 million Italians, if, through securing Rome as their national capital, the long irreligious struggle of the Papalists for temporal power should cease; he looked forward to the time when the Church, purged of worldly lusts and freed from political competition, should fulfil its mission, the mission of Christ, to sanctify and solace the souls of men. He offered it liberty, the condition through which it might thrive as never before. To Americans, accustomed for generations to the absolute separation of Church and State, and to unrestricted freedom among the churches, Cavour's proposal needs no defense. Europe, however, received it now with cynicism and now with scepticism; for Europe was too sophisticated to suppose that any body of ecclesiastics would voluntarily give up claims to power they had once possessed. Europe was too jaded by immemorial disappointments to believe that ecclesiasticism could be got rid of any more than militarism, or poverty, or the other burdens which oppressed mankind and were regarded as incurable. Some of Cavour's admirers even regretted

that he should risk being ridiculed as simple, for seeming to expect that an appeal to holy motives might stir the Roman Curia. They little knew him, whom fear of derision or of failure never deterred. The vision of the incalculable good that would come to a free Church in a free State, justified every risk. When he discussed it, Artom says, his speech became exalted to the level of poetry, and one marveled to hear him, the master economist and rational statesman, express himself with such fervor over the possible and even near accord of Catholicism and liberty.

The rebuff neither surprised nor disheartened him. "Time," he said, "is the powerful ally of him who is on the side of reason and progress." He knew that, in spite of the unmeasured conservatism inherent in human nature, dead institutions must sooner or later go to the graveyard. "Do you think the Temporal Power still exists?" he asked Artom. "The proof that it is really dead is that the occupation of Rome by the French troops fails to arouse jealousy in the other Catholic Powers. . . . It is our duty to end the long struggle between the Church and civilization, between liberty and authority. . . . Perhaps I shall be able to sign, on the summit of the Capitol, another religious peace, a treaty which will have for the future of human societies consequences far greater than those of the Peace of Westphalia. . . . It is an insult to assert that Catholicism is incompatible with liberty. I am convinced . . . that as soon as the Church has tasted liberty, she will feel herself rejuvenated by this healthful and strengthening regimen."

The immediate answer to his noble effort at conciliation came in the Pope's allocution of March 18, when he denounced progress and liberalism, and upheld the inviolability of the Temporal Power, to which he imputed a religious sanctity. His speech was the official declaration that the Roman Papacy and modern liberty were incompatible—a conclusion which the Syllabus of 1864 reaffirmed. Officially, indeed, consent would never be given to this readjustment, for the Curia never relinquishes a claim; but against facts, Rome herself can only protest: and to her protests the course of things pays no more attention, in the long run, than the comet paid to her bull. Institutions, political, social or religious, are subject to that law of growth and decay which controls not only man and every plant and animal on earth, but the life of the earth itself and the solar system, and star, and star-dust. In the presence of this universal fact, what becomes of the pretension of any church that it has not changed? Cavour no doubt instructed his agents to persuade the hierarchs that "the Papacy, which pretends to be immovable, has changed and gradually transformed itself along with Christian society. Without going back to apostolic times, one may recall that the councils offered to the nascent civilization of Europe the first model of parliamentary government. Feudal in the Middle Age, the Papacy became little by little an absolute monarchy, and thereby simply followed the general law which established the royal power as the centre of development in modern states." When the time came for democratizing monarchy, however, the Papacy could not adapt itself to the new ideals—the ossification of old age had set in. By making the great refusal at the behest of his advisers, Pius IX simply certified that the Temporal Power was dead.

EDWARD E. Y. HALES (1908–   ), an English-born Roman Catholic who taught for a while at Yale University, has written *Revolution and Papacy, 1769–1846* and other significant books on the history of the papacy and modern Italy. In this excerpt from *Pio Nono,* Hales raises a strong voice in defense of Pio Nono, as the Italians call Pope Pius IX (1846–1878), and offers an explanation of the breakdown of negotiations between Turin and Rome that is quite different from that of Thayer. According to Hales, the blame lies mostly with the Piedmontese authorities. Does he have access to more evidence than Thayer? Does religious bias seem to reveal itself in either Hales or Thayer?*

▶ ‖‖‖ *Cavour's Piedmontese Government Blamed*

With Napoleon openly unfriendly and roundly accusing the Pope of harbouring the legitimist enemies of his régime at Rome, with the British Government wholly hostile to the Temporal Power, with Austria defeated and powerless, and with the enemy at the gates of Rome there seemed no direction in which the Pope could turn even though Spain undertook a diplomatic initiative on behalf of the lesser Catholic powers and the leading French Catholic writers risked everything in issuing polemical pamphlets which pilloried the subterfuges of the Emperor's diplomacy. In these circumstances it is not surprising that there were three months, during the winter of '60–'61, when Pio Nono, though himself scorning to parley with the enemy, was prepared to allow unofficial negotiations to proceed between on the one side Cardinal Santucci, who was sympathetic with the idea of an accommodation, and on the other Fr. Passaglia, the ex-Jesuit, and his friend Diomede Pantaleoni, who were in touch with leading liberals like d'Azeglio and Mamiani. It was Pantaleoni who drew up, in November, 1860, a Memorandum embodying the idea of the renunciation by the Papacy of the

* From Edward E. Y. Hales, *Pio Nono: A Study in European Politics and Religion in the Nineteenth Century* (New York: P. J. Kenedy & Sons, 1954), pp. 221–227, omitting most of the original footnotes. Reprinted by permission of Eyre & Spottiswoode, London.

Temporal Power in return for complete independence of the Church from interference by the State. Cavour accepted the idea that Pantaleoni's Memorandum should be the basis of discussion, Passaglia agreed to show it to Cardinal Santucci, and the Cardinal showed it to the Pope, who was sufficiently interested to call in Antonelli to talk it over.

The Memorandum offered the Church material advantages. In the civil sphere the Pope would preserve the prerogatives of sovereignty, with his own diplomatic corps, complete independence from any temporal sovereign even in civil matters, ownership of the palaces, galleries and monuments traditionally belonging to the Papacy, and a regular agreed income for his court, for the Sacred College, and for the episcopate and clergy as a whole. There would be free access to Rome from the whole world. In the spiritual sphere the State would withdraw from the nomination and presentation of bishops, from interference with Papal legislation in spiritual matters—the *placet* or *exequatur* required to give state approval would thus disappear—and from all forms of inspection, or caveat. The Church would be free in the sphere of preaching, teaching, the press, and association. In its legislative and judicial function the Papacy would be able to call upon the support of the "secular arm"—e.g. in the enforcement of an interdict—but this support would be confined to the service of the Papacy; the bishops, though they would be free in their exercise of legislative and judicial power in religious matters, would not be able to call upon the secular arm to assist them.

Though Antonelli never liked the proposals, Pantaleoni succeeded in persuading Cavour that there were grounds to hope for success. Passaglia, against the wishes of Pio Nono, decided to go to Turin, where he was lodged secretly in Cavour's own house, and in February an accredited representative, Molinari (a Rosminian) was sent from Turin to negotiate at Rome on behalf of Victor Emmanuel's government. The news of Molinari's coming in this honoured capacity, at a time when most of the Papal State was under Piedmontese military occupation, and Victor Emmanuel and his ministers under the ban of excommunication, threw the Pope into one of his occasional explosions of wrath, and he declared that the envoy might be free to come to Rome but he would not be free to return. Warned of Pius' attitude Molinari was diverted at Civita-Vecchia from Rome to Naples, and soon after Pantaleoni, whose arrogant attitude and secret contacts with the revolutionaries irritated both governments, was given his passports, and the unofficial conversations were at an end.

While there had never really been much prospect of success the talks occupy an important position not merely in the evolution of the Roman Question but in the wider problem of the relations between Church and State, and in the process of "reconciling the Church with Modern Society," or with "Modern Progress," two phrases which were then becoming popular. There is no doubt that what Cavour was offering to the Church was, by contemporary Piedmontese or French standards, generous, and that he would have had plenty of trouble at Turin in persuading the Left—the followers of Rattazzi—to accept it. But his prestige at this point was such that, with the sure support of Victor Emmanuel (for whom the quarrel with Pio Nono was turning much of the pleasure of his success to bitterness), it is probable enough that he would have carried a measure of this sort in the Chamber and Senate at Turin. The accord given there to his famous speech on "a free Church in a free State" (March 27th, 1861) proves as much. It is also true that Cavour has been shown by subsequent history to have been largely right when he claimed that in a hundred years' time the relations between Church and State would normally be very much what he was advocating, no longer a régime of special privileges, whether of Church or of State, guaranteed by Concordats or Establishments, but the clearest possible distinction between the two powers. He could claim, moreover, though "more than half a Protestant," to be in line in his theory with some of the best Liberal-Catholic thought of his time, and notably with that of Montalembert, whom he was fond of quoting, even though the great French writer repudiated him with scorn;—looking at Cavour's handiwork, Montalembert called his "free Church in a free State" nothing better than a "despoiled Church in a spoliative State."

But where Cavour was most right, and Napoleon was most wrong, was in seeing that there was just a chance that Pio Nono would accept these proposals, because they were based upon a principle, whereas there was never any chance that any of the Emperor's solutions to the Roman Question, which all involved reductions in the size of the Temporal Power, and thus a mere yielding to force, would be acceptable at Rome. Cavour understood that for the Pope the issue was entirely one of principle, a matter of conscience, and that he would never yield his standpoint on the inalienability of the Temporal Power unless he could be convinced that superior spiritual advantages could be won for the Church by sacrificing it. To agree to sacrifice the Legations, or Umbria, or the Marches, would be, for the Pope, a yielding on principle. He might be compelled to see those provinces torn from him, but he would never agree that it was right that they should be; he would never recognise such a separation de jure. But if Cavour could show that he was able to offer a greater spiritual independence to the Pope and to the Church than had been secured to them through the enjoyment of the Temporal Power, then there was, indeed, some prospect of success in the negotiation, because the Pope always claimed, as his predecessors had, that the Temporal Power was necessary precisely in order to give him independence.

Why, then, did the negotiations fail? Why, when he seemed, at first, to be sympathetic, did Pio Nono end by showing more than his usual acerbity?

The reason lies in the glaring contrast between Cavour's fair words and his government's ruthless actions. It lies in the fact that during those very winter months while the conversations were proceeding the Piedmontese pro-consuls, Pepoli in Umbria, and Valerio in the Marches, were putting into operation, in the occupied provinces, the anti-clerical laws of Turin, and Mancini was extending them, in even more violent fashion, to Naples. Nobody has written with greater understanding and sympathy of Cavour's vision of a free Church in a free State than Professor Arturo Jemolo, in his recent important book Chiesa e Stato in Italia negli ultimi cento anni [(Turin, 1952), pp. 134-146]; yet the professor, who certainly holds no brief for the policies of

Pio Nono and Antonelli, has pointed out how unsound was Cavour's religious policy at this juncture:

He could well have delayed the extension of the Piedmontese ecclesiastical legislation to the annexed provinces; there would have been no harm in the convents conserving their juridical personality for a few months longer; Pantaleoni, who is certainly not to be suspected of tenderness for the cause of the religious, gave warning, on the 13th March, how difficult it was to make it acceptable at Rome that no religious corporation should have a juridical personality. Nor can it be claimed that it was simply a matter of weakness on the part of the government in the face of the party of action [the Revolutionaries]: was it not Cavour himself who, in the late autumn of '60 wrote to Pepoli, the commissioner in Umbria: 'Put into force energetic measures against the friars. You have done well to occupy some of the convents to recover there emigrants from Viterbo. Go on like that so as to heal the leprosy of monachism which infects the territories remaining under the Roman domination'?

And Professor Jemolo goes on to condemn, in particular, the arrest of Cardinal Corsi, Archbishop of Pisa, and Mgr. Ratta, of Bologna, who refused—in obedience to Rome—to allow their clergy to sing the Te Deum in honour of the anniversary of the Piedmontese constitution; arrests approved by Cavour, although recognised by him as "of little legality."[1]

Cavour was bent—desperately bent at this stage—upon securing friendship between his new Kingdom and the Church, recognising clearly enough that an accord would immeasurably improve the prospects of the precarious new state, both at home and abroad. Yet he allowed and encouraged practices which were bound to ruin the chances of this accord. It is surprising; but Cavour was liable to

make mistakes when he was handling the internal affairs of other states (notably Naples), and when he was handling people very unlike himself. He was at his best with Napoleon because his adventurous and cynical opportunism was of the same quality as that of the French Emperor. But in encouraging attacks upon the Church in the Papal State at the same time as trying to make an agreement with Pio Nono he was certainly making a serious error.

There was no reason why the anticlerical outlook of Cavour, his dislike of certain basic elements in Catholic piety, or even his personal unscrupulousness should, of themselves, have prevented Pio Nono from doing business with him. The Pope had a marked penchant for doing business with political "realists" whether they were of doubtful orthodoxy like Pellegrino Rossi, or rather materialistic, like Cardinal Antonelli, or openly Protestant, like the later French premier Émile Ollivier. But, from the time of the Siccardi Laws to the time of the occupation of most of the Papal State, the policy of Turin had been so hostile, not merely to the Temporal Power but also to the spiritual interests of the Church, that it was quite essential for Cavour's government, if Rome was to take its advances seriously, to give some evidence of a change of heart. If it didn't, of what value could any new understanding be between Church and State? It was slightly absurd to expect the Pope to hand over what

[1] Jemolo, *op. cit.*, pp. 230, 231. The verdict of another Italian historian of importance may be compared: Pio Nono's "genuine affection for Italy might well have caused him to reverse his non-possumus . . . but the religious policy of Piedmont wounded him in the very core of his being, for he was before everything else a priest." (S. F. Jacini, *La Politica Ecclesiastica Italiana da Villafranca a Porta Pia*, Bari, 1938, p. 22.)

remained to him, and especially the Eternal City, to politicians who seemed bent upon attacking and despoiling the Church. Ten years later much of the principle and the content of the Pantaleoni Memorandum was to be embodied in the Law of Guarantees, which governed the position of the Church in Italy between 1871 and the Lateran treaty of 1929; but bitter antagonism on both sides was to make its application variable and to demonstrate clearly enough that "a free Church in a free State" was not a magic formula capable of itself of dissolving all the knotty perennial problems which beset the relations between the two powers, and it was none other than religious naïveté on the part of Cavour to suppose they would melt away, even in an enlightened twentieth century, under the influence of his infallible formula.

Like Napoleon, Cavour counted upon the early death of the Pope, and the election of a more liberal successor. He did so the more readily after the events of Holy Tuesday, '61, in the Sistine Chapel, when the Pope, rising from his throne for the gospel, fell back again, and remained senseless for some minutes. It was the ensuing illness which caused Cavour to say that within six months such big changes would have taken place as would finally open to him the road to Rome.

But it was not the Pope who was about to die; it was Cavour. Seized with an intestinal infection on May 29th, '61, he died on June 6th. On June 5th he received the last sacraments from a friendly Franciscan, Fra Giacomo, who incurred the personal censure of Pio Nono for not having first exacted from the minister the formal retraction required by the Bull of Excommunication issued a year previously. Principle and personal sympathy were strangely intermingled in the reactions to this dramatic tragedy. Fra Giacomo lost his rectorship of the Church of the Madonna degli Angeli, at Turin; but he was awarded a pension of a thousand lire by a grateful government! Pio Nono, strict in upholding the law of the Church and censuring the lax priest, had yet, on first hearing of Cavour's death, raised his hands to the sky crying, "My God, be merciful with the soul of this unhappy man!" and for the repose of that soul he had duly, himself, said Mass.

It was one of the most attractive of Pio Nono's qualities that he never harboured personal animosity against any of his opponents. He always loved the sinner, while hating the sin, and he held for Cavour a personal liking, and even respect, just as he held for Victor Emmanuel a positive affection. His feeling for both men was bound up with the fact that he was, himself, such a good Italian; his quarrel with the leaders of the risorgimento was inevitable, but it did not prevent him from remaining a patriot, and being proud of it. He was proud of the fact that before any of them he had shown the way, in 1847, standing up to the Austrians and compelling them to withdraw from Ferrara; and he still loved Italy as he had loved her when he called out, in 1848, *Benedite Gran Dio l'Italia!* [Great God, bless Italy!] When Antonelli was reading him an account of Victor Emmanuel's success at Palestro, during the Austrian war of '59, he had cried, uncontrollably, *Vittorio! Vittorio! figlio mio!* [Victor! Victor! my son!], and to the astounded Cardinal he had turned and exclaimed *Per bacco! sono Italiano!* [By Jove! I am Italian!] And the diarist d'Ideville recounts how, some three years after Cavour's death, the name of the minister arose during his conversation with the Pope, whereupon:

suddenly, in a low bass voice, as though he were speaking to himself, without bothering about my presence, he murmured these words: 'Ah! How he loved his country, that Cavour, that Cavour. That man was truly Italian. God will assuredly have pardoned him as we pardon him . . .'.

And d'Ideville goes on to say how he told the story to de Mérode, who did not love the Italians, and how the war minister was annoyed, but not at all surprised by it.

So world-famed was the "idealist" philosopher-historian BENEDETTO CROCE (1866–1952) that Benito Mussolini never dared to arrest him. The Neapolitan scholar managed to show his contempt for the Blackshirt dictatorship by publishing two famous works, *A History of Italy from 1871 to 1915* (1927) and a *History of Europe in the Nineteenth Century* (1933), in both of which he reaffirmed his ardent faith in the secular "religion of liberalism" and his admiration for an era that was being denigrated by the Fascists. In the final paragraphs of his chapter on the *Risorgimento,* Croce presents a strongly favorable judgment of the liberal-nationalist movement in Italy.*

A Masterpiece of Liberal Nationalism

If it were possible in political history to speak of masterpieces as we do in dealing with works of art, the process of Italy's independence, liberty, and unity would deserve to be called the masterpiece of the liberal-national movements of the nineteenth century: so admirably does it exhibit the combination of its various elements, respect for what is old and profound innovation, the wise prudence of the statesmen and the impetus of the revolutionaries and the volunteers, ardour and moderation; so flexible and coherent is the logical thread by which it developed and reached its goal. It was called the Risorgimento, just as men had spoken of a rebirth of Greece, recalling the glorious history that the same soil had witnessed; but it was in reality a birth, a *sorgimento,* and for the first time in the ages there was born an Italian state with all and with only its own people, and moulded by an ideal. Victor Emmanuel II was right when he said, in his speech from the throne on April 2, 1860, that Italy was no longer the Italy of the Romans or of the Middle Ages, but "the Italy of the Italians."

Nor was this character, at once bold and moderate, lacking in the work of

* From Benedetto Croce, *History of Europe in the Nineteenth Century* (New York: Harcourt, Brace & Co., 1933), pp. 225–228, translated by Henry Hurst. Reprinted by permission of Agenzia Letteraria Internazionale, Milan, and George Allen & Unwin Ltd., London.

legislative and administrative and economic and financial construction of the new unitary state, which was carried out by excellent parliamentary work, principally between 1860 and 1865. And the enthusiasm was shown especially by the determination to solve the problem of the temporal power of the Papacy, of which the last but most precious remnant remained in Rome, and which was equally offensive to the national principle, as a wedge in the midst of the new state, and to the liberal consciousness, as incapable of change to civilized government. That the Papacy did not give in to these obvious national and civil arguments could not be a cause for astonishment, because the Church, a perfect society, embraces the temporal with the spiritual, and in her day extended her power far and wide, and invested and crowned the princes of the earth and excommunicated and deposed them, and if she now beheld herself reduced to ruling over a single fragment of Italy, had not for that reason given up a right that she was unable to give up without at the same time contradicting her own doctrine and nature. Not equally reasonable, nor altogether exempt from hypocrisy, were those Catholics, citizens of other states, who furiously defended the relic of temporal power in Rome—notably those French priests and bishops who used against Italy the eloquence of their pulpits as well as the attacks of their newspapers—because, in the last resort, they demanded that one single people should accomplish a duty which belonged to all Catholic peoples equally. They expected, with unchristian injustice, this one people to sacrifice its vital principles, which neither French nor Belgians nor Germans had ever sacrificed.

But even in the Papacy, except for its doctrinal premises and traditional formulas, the spirit of a Gregory VII and an Innocent III was no longer alive, and least of all in Pius IX, of whom it was said that he was decidedly lukewarm about the political thesis that he was obliged to sustain until the end by every sort of means. In diplomatic circles it was told during these years that after listening to and accepting, with the expression demanded by the occasion, the condolences and protests conveyed to him by a great German personage because of the Italian onslaughts, he had turned to someone who was standing beside him and murmured: "This German imbecile does not understand the greatness and beauty of the Italian national idea!"

The Italian parliament, cutting short the hesitation of the doubtful, defying the opposition of clericals throughout the world, with a solemn assertion of its will proclaimed Rome the capital of Italy. And through provisional transactions with France, and the renewed attempts of Garibaldi to solve the still unsolved national difficulties by the same method as that which had been used for the Two Sicilies, and the revival of the old diplomatic scheme of Louis Napoleon (from which the Italian conscience and Italian public opinion shrank) of inducing Austria to give up Venetia in exchange for Rumania, then in a grave internal crisis, thanks, last of all, to the two European wars of 1866 and 1870, the new state rounded itself out with Venetia and Rome. And here the intransigence of the Papacy permitted Italy, in the act of winning the Eternal City and making it her capital, to pull up the temporal power by the roots, not leaving to the Papacy even that little plot of ground, that minimum of a body, which, as has been observed with a Franciscan metaphor, it seems to need in order to attach its soul to it, and regulating the relations between the kingdom of Italy and the Holy See by means of a law, a monument of juridical wisdom, called the Law of Guarantees. Politically, the end of the temporal power took place amid general indifference and did not touch the other governments, of whom only a few later voiced any objections, not indeed in defence of the Papacy, but, on the contrary, because through this forcible process of spiritualization inflicted upon it by Italy, it had lost the possibility of exerting pressure upon her, in case of quarrels and conflicts. But ideally this event was, in the history of world civilization, the cancellation of the last trace of the mediaeval theocracy of the Church of Rome.

The Italian Risorgimento had been accompanied by the sympathy, the anxiety, and the admiration of the whole civilized world. The men who guided and impersonated it in the two years of the miracle, Victor Emmanuel, Cavour, Garibaldi, made a strong impression on men's imaginations, like everything that is great and extraordinary, but they also spoke to men's hearts because their significance was lifted above the particular passion of a people and stirred mankind —particularly in the poetic figure of the fighter in America, the defender of Rome, the captain of the Thousand, on whose lips the brotherhood of peoples, the peace of the nations in liberty, justice, and harmonious labour, seemed to be a living reality. To the peoples that were still labouring in difficulties and conflicts similar to those which the Italians, after so many hindrances, obstacles, and disappointments, had happily overcome, to the Germans and the Hungarians and the Poles and the other Slavs, the Italian example appeared, as may well be imagined, as a lesson, a stimulus, a renewal of sorrow, a hope, an impulse to action. The revolutionary Bakunin, echoing what they all felt and thought, wrote at this time in one of his manifestos that "from Italy's victory over Austria dated the existence in Europe of a number of nations anxious for their liberty and capable of creating a new civilization founded upon liberty." In addition to this, the fall of the old political system, in the very country where Emperor and Pope and Bourbon and Lorraine princes clung fast together in order to maintain it, and the formation of the new kingdom without disorders and revenges or other shameful and cruel things (for, as Cavour had said, liberty scorns the use in her favour of "the arms of despotism") shook the convictions of the refractory, calmed fears, relieved all tension, persuaded opponents not to persist in unwise denials, and inclined everyone to conciliation and to looking upon the liberal system with new eyes. The kingdom of Italy was recognized by the other states, even by those which were particularly conservative and authoritarian; as it was by Prussia as soon as the new king, William I, had overcome his instinctive reluctance, and in Russia by the son of Czar Nicholas, who would never have conceived the possibility of such a happening or of such recognition.

RAYMOND GREW (1930–   ) of the University of
Michigan wrote a detailed study of the manner in
which the Italian National Society recruited support
for the House of Savoy (*A Sterner Plan for Italian
Unity,* Princeton, 1963). In the following article, "How
Success Spoiled the Risorgimento," he identifies certain
opportunities for political and social reform that
were sacrificed by the Cavourian moderates during
the 1859–1860 annexation process in central Italy.
In his estimation the *Risorgimento* was a considerably
less illustrious masterpiece of liberal-nationalism
than Croce believed. Could the "errors" he cites have
been avoided by the Cavourians?*

► ‖‖‖‖ *Failed to Achieve Its Potential*

The making of a united Italy is one of the magnificent stories of the nineteenth century, and hundreds of historians have been tempted to test their prose in the telling of it. For all of them the events of 1859 and 1860 are the climax. Here the ideas of at least half a century, painted in broad, bold strokes, reach fulfilment in a series of particular events, best depicted in neat and colorful miniatures. The ideas developed during the Napoleonic experience lead to the vague yearnings of the Carbonari, the mysticism of Mazzini, and the practical program of Cavour; they are then expressed in the clash of armies, the clamor in the *piazzas* of a score of cities, Garibaldi leading his redshirts, and Cavour excitedly rubbing his hands. Perhaps it is because the story is so good that the relationship between those ideas and the particular climactic events of 1859 has been so little explored. A close analysis of their connection suggests something of crucial significance for all of modern Italian history: no one intended Italy to achieve her unification in the way she did; no one consciously wanted the political system of united Italy to be what it became. In those very months of tri-

---

* From Raymond Grew, "How Success Spoiled the Risorgimento," *The Journal of Modern History,* vol. XXXIV, no. 3 (1962), pp. 239-253. Reprinted without footnotes by permission of the author, *The Journal of Modern History,* and The University of Chicago Press.

umph, from April to December 1859, the Risorgimento itself came to be conceived in new and narrower limits.

It is too easy to see the events of 1859 marching in perfect order to the rhythmic needs of a narrative. The volunteers streaming across the Ticino show the growing enthusiasm for unification and provoke Austria into rash hostility. After an agonizing moment of uncertainty, war is declared; and the French prove true to their word. Revolutions then sweep across the Duchies and into the Romagna, extending the war and displaying a unanimity of popular sentiment that is itself the climax of years of propaganda and daring. In contrast to those of 1848, however, these revolutions are bloodless, and they succeed. The provisional governments which replace the departed dukes then do the work of destiny by subordinating themselves to the agents of Cavour. Suddenly, hopes are dashed as the Truce of Villafranca ends the war, providing merely for the addition of Lombardy to the Piedmontese domains, but Italy's nationalists remain steadfast. The provisional regimes in Tuscany, the Duchies, and the Romagna maintain order and earnestly adopt Piedmontese coinage and tariffs. They hold assemblies where, with happy unanimity, the demand is made for their annexation by Piedmont. In effect, Europe is presented with a *fait accompli,* the accomplishment of rare restraint. The dark hour of Cavour's resignation has proved to be a new dawn. Northern Italy, save Venice, becomes one country. Cavour's policy has triumphed after all.

Seen in this light, the political events in Italy from the outbreak of the war to the end of 1859 are a mere supplement to the drama of the war itself and a logical extension of Cavour's general policy. Such a view is not wrong, although it tends inevitably to a somewhat unhistorical tone, but it is inadequate. It treats the Risorgimento as the contagion of a common sentiment rather than as a multiform political movement concerned with real and important issues. It misses the point that while skilfully conducting this campaign Italy's leaders were, without meaning to and certainly without facing the fact, doing much to determine what the politics of united Italy would be like. It was during this period of fulfilment that the Risorgimento became a movement which largely eliminated the masses from participation in politics. So conceived, it discouraged the discussion of those political questions which had been its substance. It restricted to a minimum those political and social changes which had been its promise. Administrative fiat and dictatorship became the means for making decisions.

The narrowing of popular participation in the movement to unify Italy began before the war. The volunteers who made their way to Piedmont that spring provided the greatest demonstration of Italian political consciousness in ten years. Nearly 20,000 had arrived by March; yet the leaders of Piedmont were never comfortable with this exciting sign of the success of their policies. They had suggested that those men being conscripted into Austrian or local Italian armies come to serve in Piedmont instead, thinking, with somewhat exaggerated realism, that these would be the only ones likely to come. There was, however, a graver reason for that suggestion: those avoiding conscription would be soldiers first and political demonstrators second. Volunteers, in contrast, were notoriously susceptible to infectious ideologies and were likely to be more loyal to Garibaldi than to formal military discipline. Thus the government remained ambivalent in its attitude toward these men, mostly students and not such a motley crew after all, who in increasing numbers slipped across the borders to prove, through the risks they took, their personal courage and their confidence in Piedmont. These and the other reasons, domestic and diplomatic, for the government's hesitance are easily understood. This was a movement that created an atmosphere of chaos. It was one that might easily get out of hand and begin to define its own political goals. It might even produce an unfortunate revolt across the Ticino or in the Duchies. The hesitance those reasons produced meant that the leading state in Italy could not support the demonstration of widespread belief in its leadership, that the opportunity to make a more popular movement of its policy had to be missed, that the war of Italian liberation would be a battle of professional armies, that neither the popularity of Garibaldi nor the political and military potentialities of the thousands ready to rally to him could be effectively used.

The same sort of fear prevented the moderates from advocating local insurrections in the spring of 1859. The war plans of the previous year had included local revolts both as the war's justification and as a device for extending it outside Lombardy. Yet these plans, so precise in 1858, became increasingly vague as the time came to use them. The National Society, which still thought of itself as the agent of revolution, shared all of Cavour's concern that revolt might break out too soon, either fail or spread too far, endanger the diplomatic security of Piedmont or allow more radical forces to triumph locally and then use their position to modify Piedmont's. When at last the National Society issued the call to revolt, it was muffled and faint. The moderates had turned from revolution; they preferred to have Italy's fortunes decided with the more limited risks of battle.

No real revolution occurred in Italy in 1859, no popular participation in government as in 1848. The revolt in Milan was a calm transference of powers, directed in part by an agent of Cavour immediately after the departure of the Austrians. A revolution might have taken place in Tuscany if the grand duke had not left before anything more serious than a demonstration was necessary. Again an ambassador of Cavour, Carlo Boncompagni, and the Tuscan moderates kept things well in hand so that the complications of unneeded enthusiasm were avoided. In Modena and the Romagna, too, the nationalists rose only as the Austrians left. Marco Minghetti, who was one of those closest to Cavour, had seen such cautious waiting as a means whereby the Romagna could avoid the "political question," a strange goal for a revolution. These were rather *coups d'état,* and, in contrast to the National Society's premature attempt in Parma, they relied on the proximity of Piedmontese troops. Minghetti was relieved that his country's future would now be "the necessary consequence of great happenings" and "no longer the work of any party." Politics as the public discussion of the form and methods of government was to be avoided.

In each town a faint legality was maintained, as the existing city council appointed a provisional government of moderate nationalists. The provisional governments tended to see their function as an extension of diplomacy. They were to do what Piedmont alone dared not, replace the previous government and then hand their authority to Victor Emmanuel. Thus any opposition, diplomatic or domestic, was faced with that surest of political weapons, the accomplished fact. Wherever possible the treaties of 1848 were re-invoked, and with little concern for the legality of their mandate the provisional governments then handed the full powers they claimed to a commissioner of Piedmont. Usually within a week an agent of Cavour exercised the full political power of the province. And Cavour's followers, in or out of office, tended to accept in the name of freedom the gravest restrictions on its practice. They could, like a group about to found a newspaper in Tuscany, volunteer for censorship believing that there would come "a time of free discussions"; and they expected a similar "sacrifice" from their more radical opponents. It is not surprising that under the new dispensation radicals and Mazzinians found they had no more rights in theory and perhaps fewer in practice, partly because the efficient men of the new government knew so well who the Mazzinians were.

But when the talk of the political and social changes which the Risorgimento must bring about had lessened, so did the pressure for reform. After their patriotic addresses to Victor Emmanuel and their somewhat fawning ones to Napoleon III, the provisional governments had made it a point to make few changes. The exigencies of war supported their own political desire to avoid controversy, and the provisional government of Tuscany spoke for them all when it declared

that any reordering of institutions should be postponed until the "great enterprise is completed." Such postponement ran the risk, of course, of becoming permanent; but to men determined to avoid the errors of 1848 it appeared a "sacred duty" to avoid "untimely innovations." The provisional government in Milan had shown its doctrinal liberalism by abolishing the death penalty, declaring the civil equality of Jews, and allowing political exiles to return. The *giunta* in Bologna did these things, too, and even reduced tariffs and adopted the Napoleonic Code while demonstrating its reliable hardheadedness by prohibiting all newspapers and political writings from its first day in power. Yet the old bureaucracy was maintained, and the police little altered. Indeed, it had to be explained to the public by proclamation that these institutions of former repression had, with few changes even in personnel, now become trustworthy. Except for such brief flurries of activity, the Piedmontese commissioners found themselves presented with full powers essentially unlimited by the preceding acts of the provisional governments; and Cavour's men, Boncompagni, Luigi Carlo Farini, Diodato Pallieri, and Massimo d'Azeglio, made appointments to major administrative posts and picked their own advisers with surprisingly little regard for those who had so happily handed the reins to them. When the provisional governments dissolved, the moderates of daring quickly gave way to still milder moderates of greater respectability.

The changes they tended to institute were not those evoked by visions of a better society but those which resulted from administrative need. The extensive authority given the commissioners had a precedent in the granting of dictatorship to Victor Emmanuel, a step which had on all sides been regarded as essential, so much so that to suggest constitutional guarantees in the interim seemed an affront to the *Re Galantuomo*. This authority came to be wielded by others who, in his name and with doubtful constitutionality, limited the freedom of the press, applied the penal code, prorogued parliament, levied tariffs and taxes. It is a tribute to the probity of these provincial dictators that this power was not more seriously misused. But the constitutional precedents were dangerous, and the procedures used were often unfortunate. Piedmontese laws were extended by fiat without either theoretical concern for their merits or careful study of local conditions. It was in Lombardy that the processes of bureaucracy first began to deal (as they would later in the rest of Italy) with some of the crucial issues no assembly had discussed. The Piedmontese court system was extended there by decree; the new penal code, with its dangerously complex clauses on religious liberty, was announced, and the limited local government to be allowed in Lombardy was defined. Even these laws were often violated in practice, and the new Italian state experienced from the first some of the censorship and arbitrary imprisonment that had been familiar under other regimes. But the pattern for Italy's administration was set. It would be highly centralized and ruled by Piedmontese codes which protected liberty with few fundamental guarantees.

After the truce at Villafranca, these regimes were no longer directly supported by the power of Piedmont, and the commissioners turned their authority over to the local leaders with whom they had been working. These provincial governments then had to secure a popular sanction, and soon each of them followed Farini's lead from Modena in calling for elections to provincial "national assemblies." The suffrage, which varied in the different provinces, was announced by decree. With some pride it was usually added that the elections would in fact be free, although Baron Bettino Ricasoli included the warning that those who dared disturb the concord of Tuscans would be punished. Prefects were instructed to take a "beneficent initiative" in the naming of candidates in order that the election would not be "pre-empted by parties," and to encourage the political dominance of reliable citizens. Still, the prefects were expected to act at least with decorum; and the voting appears not to have been outrageously rigged.

When they met, the provincial assemblies showed the implications of politics which narrowed the popular participation in Italy's unification, eschewed (and often prevented) political discussion, ignored the aspirations for reform, and depended so heavily on administrative fiat. The records of those assemblies, which provide an insight into the attitudes of the men so earnestly pursuing Cavourian policies, have been largely neglected by historians. They reveal that those conventions were deliberative bodies only in form.

Despite the hint of democratic aspirations in their titles, these national assemblies were notable for their abnegation. Each of them declared the downfall of the old regime after minimal discussion and by a unanimous vote. But they treated those regimes as if they had abdicated rather than as if they had been overthrown and pictured themselves as preventing anarchy rather than making a revolution. The somewhat miscellaneous lists of their former rulers' failings which were drawn up in the assemblies avoided any theoretical justification for the most important and permanent political change in modern Italian history. The assemblies chose Victor Emmanuel to be their king and maintained the interim regimes; but impressed, as astute men were bound to be, with the role of foreign affairs in determining Italy's fate, they conducted themselves like diplomats rather than legislators (thus the excessive encomiums of Louis Napoleon). They were carrying out a demonstration rather than fulfilling a natural right. They therefore expected unanimous votes. And nearly every vote, whether secret or open, was unanimous; indeed, the favorite argument for voting secretly was that this would make a better demonstration, while without such secrecy a negative vote might be recorded by mistake. Only in Tuscany and Parma was there ever anything approaching debate. Yet in Tuscany, where regional pride was strong, so important a question as whether the new Italian state should be a federation was dismissed as "too vast, too complex, and . . . too academic, to be unfolded before this Assembly." In Parma the Piedmontese *Statuto* was adopted with no discussion of its merits.

This is what the emphasis on "concord" was coming to mean; Farini made it clear in his address to the assemblies in Modena and Parma. "Concord," he said, "has been until now our greatest strength, but this concord is composed of elements which, united in their ultimate and highest end, are nevertheless

diverse by their nature." It was, he implied, only the pressure of European politics which had kept such diversity from flying apart (he was becoming grateful for the limitations of circumstance). With disarming clarity he added that the great difficulty had been for so long a time to hold their movement within the "limits traced by cold reason of state." It was the importance of maintaining just those limits that D'Azeglio had in mind when he declared, on taking charge in Bologna: "If you know how to obey, you will know how to fight and win." He added that discipline and order had no roots where discords flamed. And when he departed, he warned the Romagnols: "One single danger menaces you: discord and disorder." In all the assemblies, the deputies frequently asserted that they were not revolutionaries. They said that not merely to put the British and French at ease; they were reassuring themselves. They sensed that they wanted little change; they knew that by limiting discussion they would be safer from the dangers both of change and of dissension. Faced with nearly all the major issues of nineteenth-century politics at once, they hoped to postpone the controversial ones.

II

The manner and tone of the politics of a united Italy were being determined, but the followers of Cavour who dominated those politics in 1859 took pride in being pragmatists. If in a sequence of crises their practices whittled away at their own liberal vision of the Risorgimento, they were scarcely aware of it. The interaction of ideas and events is always subtle, but the effect of that subtlety in this case is easily overlooked because the methods employed by Cavour's followers and the political system they created are, when seen with hindsight, so easily explained by calling these men "moderates." In this period the term was usually reserved for those like Cavour, Minghetti, Farina, Ricasoli, or perhaps D'Azeglio, who by the 1850's had come to dominate Italian politics—for those who were politically influential, decently nationalist, and loyally monarchist.

Often members of the aristocracy or at least men who could move with ease in such circles, these followers of Cavour had become reformers in the Enlightenment tradition of scientific societies and agricultural associations. They had discovered, like Cavour, that successful pig farming required political reform. Often they had, like Minghetti with Pius IX, tried to work within the old regimes. Finding themselves stifled there, and touched by the Mazzinian dream, they came to think in more than provincial terms. Yet they felt a deep distaste for revolution, and it was easy for them to lead Italians in learning from the failures of 1848. They found a pattern for reform without revolution in the contemporary history of England and France, models made natural for them by their own international connections. Thus the moderates tended to advocate representative institutions while remaining suspicious of politics and contemptuous of parties, for they had learned from Antonio Rosmini that parties are "worms which devour the fabric of society." They adopted liberal economic theory and believed in the importance and inevitability of economic growth. Here they most directly appealed to Italy's small middle class of merchants and lawyers. Combining a respect for the traditional institutions of power (such as the monarchy and the military) with demands for change, they easily adopted the tone of realism and naturally shared the fears of a Lord Malmesbury.

Finally, they were compromisers who were keenly aware of the weakness of their position; for compromise, as a principle, makes the dullest of political programs. Mazzini could fail and maintain a following. The moderates were certain they must succeed in winning much of what the nationalists wanted whenever they had the chance or lose their dominance. That conviction both stimulated their courage and increased their caution. It explains Cavour's panic that the war might not begin in April and his famous loss of temper on learning the news of Villafranca. These displays of emotion were not, as often interpreted, merely signs of an uncharacteristic flaw or uncontrolled patriotism. For the moment Cavour's policy had failed, and out of Mazzini's steady flow of prognostications, dire and utopian, the warnings against an alliance with France stood out as apparently proved. Yet the Cavourian policy did not collapse, and the Risorgimento contains no greater testimonial to the sagacity of the Moderates than their conduct of Italian affairs in the months following Villafranca.

The Moderates thought of themselves as liberal as well as nationalist, but the methods they employed in 1859 had done much to make a liberal state less likely. Like their ideological cousins elsewhere in Europe, Italian moderates had run too far from the failures of 1848. Determined to avoid fatal political divisions, they had sought unanimity less through agreement than by postponing all "lesser" issues, all questions but unification. Postponement in practice proved to be decision without discussion. Determined this time to succeed, they had stressed the military virtues of discipline and order. The very concepts of unification and liberty had been vigorously and deliberately separated as distinct issues unnecessarily cumbersome when taken together.

Only a program which took advantage of the ambitions of Piedmont, the aims of the lower middle class, and the discontents of the lower middle and artisan classes could have won widespread support. Only one with which Louis Napoleon could associate himself and which Great Britain could accept was likely to succeed. The moderates, with only occasional slips, provided that program. To do so, however, they expressed ideas which were the critique of the policies they pursued. They sounded like Gladstone but performed like Guizot. Confident there was a law of progress, the moderates believed they had opened Italy to its beneficial effects. They could rely on time to correct their omissions.

The moderates' policies in these exciting months of 1859 are important to historical understanding, then, for a number of reasons. Those policies succeeded, and they established the kind of political system under which united Italy operated: a highly centralized state dominated by the bureaucracy with effective power limited to a small group of men with similar backgrounds and interests. Those policies are important, too, precisely because what the moderates did was not what they had advocated. To begin with, a great deal about the kind of Risorgimento they would direct

had not been determined by the spring of 1859. The moderates themselves did not know whether the war would extend to the Papal States, Sicily, or even to Tuscany; there was little deliberation about the role revolutions might play. Even the old hope for something like a constituent assembly to follow a successful war had not been clearly rejected. As enemies of Mazzini, the moderates had denounced his tactics and condemned his means; but they had not, even in their own thinking, altogether divorced themselves from his vision of the future. In August Farini could still insist that a united Italy would not be centralized *alla francese,* and Minghetti years later would not understand the impossibility of fulfilling that promise.

More important, the moderates were both deeply nationalist and devoted to the concept of parliamentarism. The very assemblies which so avoided debate had medals struck for the men who had volunteered and monuments built to commemorate the actions of the populace. Perhaps it was the implications of social unity within nationalism which the moderates understood best, but they did not shun the suggestion of domestic freedom which was part of the meaning of independence. The moderates were fond of the word "liberty," and they had freely promised it as the fruit of their labors. For them a national parliament was the very symbol of unification; justice through law was the highest achievement of the state. In the chamber of deputies or in the various assemblies they expected their representative institutions to be treated with respect, and they took delight in parliamentary procedures. They espoused liberal economic theories which implied social changes that, in the Italy of the 1850's, were in fact revolutionary. Their deviations from such programs they saw only as the result of practical necessity. But their very practicality made it difficult for them to see how far they had strayed from such abstract standards and made it impossible for them to understand the charge that they had moved always in the direction of their immediate class interests.

This is why to their opponents the moderates seemed cynical, and why the charge of bad faith added such anguish to Italian political disputes. When Garibaldi resigned from the army in the autumn of 1859, the conflicts in political views so long suppressed or ignored began to appear. Enforced inactivity had proved too much for him, and, with public bitterness, he destroyed the illusion that Italian nationalists were happily co-operating. Yet Garibaldi had been too much influenced by the cry for "concord" to assume a clear political position. He expressed, rather, his frustrated activism and the dangerous contempt for politics which often marked his views, allowing himself to be used by a political opposition with clearer goals. The moderates, on the other hand (especially with Cavour out of office), did not realize how secure their position was. Having for long tended to see parties as a manifestation of the selfishness of their opponents, they reacted with anger instead of the generous tolerance their position justified. The split between the National Society and the *Liberi Comizii* and between Cavour and Garibaldi became bitter, deep, and open.

As eminently practical men, the moderates reflected with some sensitivity the political pressures of their time. Their policy was formed by the nature of the domestic as well as the diplomatic scene. And this makes an understanding of what the moderates did of further importance to the historian. They did not distort the truth when they acted as if the middle class was weak and assumed that there was no clear popular pressure for any specific program opposed to theirs. Indeed, they were probably right in viewing themselves as the only ones capable of unifying Italy. Even their convinced opponents found it difficult to make a clear and politically effective critique of their policy. With all their skill Angelo Brofferio and Agostino Bertani could not. They sensed that Cavourian policies were stranding the nationalists of the Left with no alternative but to acquiesce in the moderates' triumph or withdraw from politics. By the autumn of 1859, they were indignant but frustrated. They tended to share the moderates' impatience with "detail" which prevented a careful formulation of alternative policies, and they made their criticism in terms of moral categories which could too easily be made to seem unconnected with political reality. Most enfeebling of all, these opponents of Cavour were themselves impressed by success. Despite their sincerity, they betrayed the poverty of their position as they returned again and again to an ill-defined mystique of revolution.

Finally, taken all together, these policies the moderates so practically pursued during the triumphant months of 1859 played their part in much of subsequent Italian history. The way in which Italy was united left a dull, persistent ache in the Italian body politic. The exclusion from politics of most Italians was part of that legacy. Garibaldi came to represent the participation through direct action of those who had been left out. It was this which made him seem a threat to Cavour in 1860 and caused the prime minister to view the general with such harsh fear. The tendency to substitute men proved in Piedmont for local leaders (including even those who had been active in the National Society), the split with Garibaldi, the intolerance toward the parliamentary Left (and the habit of seeing in it all the dangers of the Parisian proletariat) led to the narrowing of the political base of the new Italy. This was a moment, however, at which the urban lower middle class and some leading artisans were gaining a new political self-consciousness. When years later they were admitted to effective political life, they tended first to fight the battle of their past deprivation. Italy's political base was not broad enough to support a system of two parties, while the exclusion of democrats and Catholics left an increasingly isolated ruling caste. And the beleaguered, earnest moderates could not forget the moments of unanimity they had claimed in 1859; for them, disagreement would always smack of a selfish partisanship, a decline from the greatness of Cavour's age.

"Unconditional unitarianism" one of the moderates' opponents labeled this attitude, in arguing that inherently it led to the sacrifice of liberty. But that tendency was the more dangerous because united Italy suffered from the lack of traditions of legality and precedents of restraint. These shortcomings, too, were part of the legacy of moderate policy. One could not effectively cite the authority of constitution and laws when they were the product neither of some dominant ideology nor of a publicly welded compromise. They had been ex-

pedients, so tightly tied to the needs of the moment that they lost dignity as circumstances changed. They had been weakened from the first by the reliance on dictatorship in Piedmont and in the provinces. It would remain a temptation, as in the plebiscites of 1860, to use the instruments of representative government primarily for safe demonstrations which left a slight sense of sham. Urbano Rattazzi was only the first of a long line of lesser successors to be tempted by Cavour's gaudier successes. Well before Aspromonte or the days of Agostino Depretis, he had done his part in 1859 to make corridor intrigue and the extra constitutional support of the king an important part of Italian politics. Too often diplomatic triumphs would seem, as they had in 1859 but with more reason, the only way of overcoming domestic division. And in the decade after 1860 parliament was plagued, in addition to its regular burdens, by the need to serve as the constituent assembly which had not been held. It is no wonder that the new legal codes were exceedingly cautious and inappropriately close to their French models. They, too, became a source of disappointment and dissatisfaction.

Disappointment was deepened by the fact that, in the process of achieving national union, nationalism itself had been somewhat tainted. Caution and realism had led, in 1859, to that regional self-interest which made Tuscany hesitant to join with the Duchies and both of them reluctant to associate their claims to the diplomatically dangerous ones of the Romagna. The Perugian patriots had been abandoned; and if, in a few bloody days, they had displayed the weakness of revolution, they had established, too, the unheroic limits of Piedmontese realism. The cession of Nice was another of those bitter blows to the sanguine nationalist, a list of which could easily be extended to 1866. Many of these disappointments are a measure of how weak the forces were which worked for Italy's union. Indeed, an assessment of the difficulties the moderates faced suggests that unification was neither so inevitable nor so imminent as most contemporaries thought. In this sense, the moderates accomplished more than they could claim. But the discovery of what unification did not achieve led to the recognition of what narrow aims moderates had. When coupled with the assumption that Italian unification was a nineteenth-century necessity, it led to the feeling that the moderates had been guilty of some subtle treachery, of having stolen something.[1]

But by far the most important legacy of the moderate policy was the disappointment in the Risorgimento, in Italy itself, which grew to haunt Italian politics. The discontent with Piedmontese laws, the sense of having been cheated out of the old dream of a constituent assembly arose even before the new state was established and spread as a criticism of the foundation of the regime. Inevitably the Left lamented the fall from its ideals, but even the conservative Alfonso La Marmora confessed a decade later that the means by which Italy had been made embarrassed those who later governed. Much of the caution of 1859 had been meant to reassure Europe, but even this could be self-defeating. With self-righteous perceptiveness the *Westminster review* complained at the time that the Italians had shown "more sagacity than energy," that their freedom had been won "by a fortunate deficiency of ve-

hemence and excitement." Italy's dependence on other countries had been made too clear; and these things, like the limited role granted the provisional governments, deprived the successful Risorgimento of 1859 of the heroic tradition of its predecessor. The famous post-unification political apathy was more than a letdown once the one great goal was achieved. It expressed a sense of disappointment with the past as well as the present. The feeling of the revolution *manquée* was born with the successes of 1859, and Boncompagni confessed more than he meant when, in 1871, he noticed that Italy was "more fortunate than great."

While the attention of all concerned was concentrated on the skill and luck with which political unification was at last being achieved in Italy, the meaning of that unification was being determined with far less attention. The moderates were almost pathetically eager to establish that Italians could behave with the popular restraint and political responsibility of Englishmen and Frenchmen. And that rather limited aim they attained. But in doing so they bore the burden not only of Italy's history but of their neighbors' as well. They could have been more generous to the classes beneath them if they had not confused them with the more demanding masses of the industrialized countries. They could have won a wider following if their opponents had not had ready at hand all the argu-

[1] The moderates were by temperament as well as program ill-equipped to excite the popular imagination. The perceptive young Henry Adams predicted at the time that Italy would "adore Garibaldi's memory, and only respect Cavour's" (letter to his brother, Charles Francis, June 9, 1860, "Henry Adams and Garibaldi," *American historical review*, XXV [1919–20], 248).

ments against Whiggish limitations developed in the different context of Britain and France. What was done in 1859 is explicable in terms of the needs then felt and understandable in terms of the values the moderates held; and by so assessing it, one can escape the traditional polemics. The crucial months of 1859 stand, then, as something of a turning point; but their historical importance lies more deeply in the opportunity they afford for studying the ideals and realities of the Risorgimento. What was then done, when every act was a political decision, teaches something about the balance of forces in Italy as well as the weaknesses of that practical liberalism so common to the nineteenth century. As for the deeds themselves, one need only ponder them to recognize within the exciting story the importance of the precedents then set and of the pride Italian patriots could not feel in a country so compromisingly formed.

Taking advantage of the failure of most Crocean historians to interest themselves in socioeconomic problems, Italian communist historians have established a bridgehead in this field. They follow suggestions for a Marxian class-struggle historical interpretation laid down in notebooks secretly kept in a Fascist prison by their party founder, ANTONIO GRAMSCI (1891–1937). According to him, the *Risorgimento* was an agrarian *rivoluzione mancata*. Gramsci criticizes the Action Party (the Mazzinian-Garibaldian forces) for not exploiting allegedly widespread agrarian unrest in the way the Jacobins did during the French Revolution.*

▶ # *Neglected Agrarian Revolution*

The problem of political leadership in the formation and development of the nation and the modern state in Italy:

The whole problem of the connection between the various political currents of the *Risorgimento*—that is to say, of their relationships with each other and with the homogeneous or the stratified social groups in the various historical sections of the national territory—reduces itself to these essential facts:

The moderates represented a social group that was relatively homogeneous. For that reason, their leadership under-went relatively slight modifications (and, in any case, they followed an organically progressive line of development). The so-called Action Party, on the other hand, did not rest specifically on any single historical class, and the oscillations that took place within its executive organs corresponded in the final analysis to the interests of the moderates. In other words, historically, the Action Party was guided by the moderates. Thus the affirmation attributed to Victor Emmanuel II of having the Action Party "in his pocket," or something like that, is true for all practical purposes, and not simply

* From Antonio Gramsci, *Il Risorgimento* (Turin: Giulio Einaudi Editore, 1949), pp. 69–70, 72, 73, 81–82, 87–88, 103–104, omitting some of the footnotes. Translated by Charles F. Delzell. Reprinted by permission of the Istituto Gramsci, Rome, and Giulio Einaudi, Turin.

107

because the Action Party was in fact led "indirectly" by Cavour and the King. . . .

For the Action Party to have become an autonomous force and, in the final analysis, to have succeeded at least in imprinting upon the *Risorgimento* movement a character that was more distinctly popular and democratic (more than this it perhaps could not do, in view of the fundamental premises of the movement itself), it should have countered the "empirical" activity of the moderates . . . with an organic program of government that reflected the essential demands of the popular masses, above all, of the peasants. It should have countered the "spontaneous" attraction exercised by the moderates with a resistance and an "organized," planned counteroffensive. . . .

Actually, the Action Party completely lacked a specific governmental program. More than anything else, it remained essentially in the service of the moderates as an organism for agitation and propaganda. The internal conflicts of the Action Party, the tremendous hatreds against Mazzini and his work that Mazzini aroused in the sturdiest Actionists (Garibaldi, Felice Orsini, and others) were caused by the absence of firm political leadership. The internal polemics were in large measure as abstract as the preaching of Mazzini had been. Yet one can draw useful historical lessons from them. (Of importance for everyone are the writings of [Carlo] Pisacane, who committed, however, irreparable political and military errors, such as opposing Garibaldi's military dictatorship in the Roman Republic.) The Action Party was intoxicated by the traditional rhetoric of Italian literature. It confused the cultural unity of the peninsula (a unity that was confined to a very narrow stratum of the population and was besmirched by the Vatican's cosmopolitanism) with a feeling of political and territorial unity on the part of the great popular masses, who actually stood quite apart from that cultural tradition and did not care about it, even when they knew of its existence. . . .

From these observations and analyses of several elements in Italian history after unification, one can form certain criteria for appreciating the contrasting positions of the moderates and the Action Party, and for discovering the diverse political "wisdom" of these two parties and of the various currents that fought for political and ideological leadership of the [Action Party]. In order to counter the moderates effectively, it is evident that the Action Party should have attached itself to the rural masses, especially in the south. It should have been "Jacobin" not only in external "form" and temperament, but above all in its economic and social program. Only by pushing forward in two directions could it have forestalled the consolidation of the various rural classes into a reactionary bloc, then being forged by legitimist and clerical intellectual cliques, and make room for a new liberal, national formation. [It should have pushed forward] (1) toward the peasants at the bottom, accepting their basic demands and making them an integral part of the new program of government; and (2) toward the intellectuals of the medium and lower strata, binding them together and insisting upon the themes that might interest them most. (Already the prospect of the formation of a new apparatus of government, with the possibility of employment therein, was a great attraction to them, if the prospect could be presented concretely on the basis of the aspirations of the rural population.)

The relationship between these two courses of action was dialectical and reciprocal. The experience of many countries—and above all that of France during the period of the great Revolution—shows that whenever the peasants act for "spontaneous" reasons, the intellectuals begin to waver. Conversely, if a group of intellectuals espouse a new program of specifically pro-peasant politics, they end by pulling along with them ever more important segments of the population. We can say, however, that in view of the dispersal and isolation of the rural population and the resulting difficulty of concentrating it in solid organizations, the movement must be initiated by means of intellectual groups. In general, however, it is the dialectical relationship between the two courses of action that must be kept in mind. One might add that it is almost impossible to create peasant parties in the strict sense of the term. The peasant party usually emerges only as a strong current of opinion, not in the well worked-out form of bureaucratic cadres. Nevertheless, the existence of even a skeletal organization is immensely useful, both in bringing about a certain solution to the leadership problem and in controlling intellectual groups and preventing caste interests from guiding them imperceptibly into new fields. . . .

The reasons why no Jacobin party was formed in Italy are to be sought in the economic field—that is, in the relative weakness of the Italian bourgeoisie and in Europe's different historical climate after 1815. Even though the Le Chapelier Law and the Law of the Maximum had limited the Jacobin program of seeking by force to reawaken the energies of the French popular masses so as to ally them with the bourgeoisie, the program still appeared in 1848 as a threatening "specter," and this fact was cleverly exploited by Austria and the old governments, even by Cavour—to say nothing of the pope. Perhaps because of subjective (though not objective) factors, the bourgeoisie could no longer extend its hegemony over as wide a range of common people [in Italy] as it had in France; nevertheless, activity among the peasantry was certainly always possible.

The relationship between city and countryside in the Risorgimento and in the national structure:

. . . Why did the Action Party fail to make an issue of the agrarian question in all its ramifications? The reason why the moderates did not is obvious. The terms of reference that the moderates assigned to the national problem necessitated a bloc of all rightist forces, including the great landed proprietors who would group themselves around the state and army of Piedmont. Austria's threat to resolve the agrarian question in favor of the peasants (a threat that had been carried out in Galicia against the Polish nobility, in favor of the Ruthenian peasants) threw dismay into the ranks of interested property owners in Italy and caused the wavering among the aristocrats. (The disorders of February 1853 in Milan and the paying of homage to [Emperor] Francis Joseph by Milan's most illustrious families occurred on the eve of the Belfiore atrocity.[1]) Moreover, the agrarian question paralyzed the Ac-

[1] In March 1853 nine Italians were executed on the bastions of Belfiore in Mantua after being convicted of possession of anti-Austrian literature and raising money for an Italian revolt.—*Ed.*

tion Party itself, which on this subject thought the same way as the moderates, regarding only the aristocracy and property owners as "nationalists," not the millions of peasants. Only after February 1853 did Mazzini make any substantially democratic references (see his *Epistolario* [Correspondence] for that period), but he was incapable of giving a decisively radical slant to his abstract program.

We should study too the political behavior of the *garibaldini* in Sicily in 1860, a political policy that was dictated by [Francesco] Crispi. The insurrectionary movements of the [Sicilian] peasants against the barons were pitilessly suppressed, and an anti-peasant National Guard was created. The repressive expedition of Nino Bixio in the Catania region where the insurrections were most violent was typical. Yet, even in the *Noterelle* [Diary] of G. C. Abba we find evidence that the agrarian question was the spring that was coiled to set the great masses into motion. It is enough to recall Abba's conversation with the monk who went to talk to the *garibaldini* right after their landing at Marsala.[2] And in several stories by G. Verga there is picturesque evidence of this peasant unrest, which the National Guard stifled by means of terror and mass executions. This aspect of the expedition of the Thousand has never been studied and analyzed.

The failure to face up to the agrarian question led to the near impossibility of resolving the question of clericalism and of the pope's antiunification attitude. In this regard the moderates were much bolder than the Action Party. True, they did not distribute ecclesiastical holdings among the peasants. However, they used such holdings to create a new class of large and medium property owners who were linked to the new political order, and they did not hesitate to liquidate land holdings, even though these involved only property belonging to the Congregations. The Action Party was paralyzed in its attitude toward the peasantry, moreover, by illusory Mazzinian dreams of a religious Reformation—a goal that not only failed to interest the great mass of rural people but made them susceptible to reactionary moves against the new heretics. . . .

[2] Gramsci's allusion is to the diary entry of May 22, 1860, by Giuseppe Cesare Abba, one of Garibaldi's Redshirts. Abba was flabbergasted by the social revolutionary comments of the friar. The monk intimated that if Garibaldi would launch a truly socioeconomic revolution and carry the Bible and cross before him, he would himself join forces with him. First published in 1880, Abba's *Noterelle* achieved widespread fame in Italy. It is now available in an English translation by E. R. Vincent as *The Diary of One of Garibaldi's Thousand* (London: Oxford University Press, 1962).—*Ed.*

One of the few Crocean-trained historians to shift his research interests to the socioeconomic problems of Italy's south is ROSARIO ROMEO (1924–   ), author of a ground-breaking study, *Il Risorgimento in Sicilia* (1950). A few years after completing that work this liberal, capitalist historian wrote two essays dealing with recent Marxian historiography in Italy and his own theory of how industrial development after 1861 actually was stimulated by the unreformed agrarian structure. This passage comes from the first of the essays. In it Romeo argues that Gramsci anachronistically sought to transfer the Communist Party's twentieth-century program into the past. In short, objective conditions for an agrarian revolution simply did not exist in 1860. Romeo has contributed to a debate that shows no sign of ending soon.*

Liberal-Capitalist Rebuttal to Gramsci's Thesis

[Italian] Marxist historiography during the past decade has concerned itself primarily with the history of the *Risorgimento* and the unified state. And this historiography is almost entirely focused on the noted thesis that the *Risorgimento* was an agrarian *rivoluzione mancata*—a thesis generally known as the "Gramsci thesis."

Attributing this thesis to Gramsci is a bit arbitrary and in part inexact. We mention this not to raise an abstract question as to its paternity—for in this respect the label may very well be adopted, as we certainly owe to Gramsci the most coherent and profound formulation of the thesis—but to point out an important element in it, an element that tends to be relegated to the background when it is attributed solely to Gramsci. In reality, the immediate post-World War II period saw the first explicit formulation of criticism of the bourgeoisie of the *Risorgimento* era for not broadening their national movement into a more consolidated democratic, bourgeois revolution that might also have mobilized the peasant masses for the purpose of overthrowing and eliminating the remnants of feudalism in the countryside.

---

* From Rosario Romeo, "La tesi del Gramsci e il problema dello sviluppo del capitalismo," in *Risorgimento e capitalismo* (Bari, Italy: Editori Laterza, 1959), pp. 17-24, 45-46, omitting the original footnotes. Translated by Charles F. Delzell. Reprinted with the permission of Editori Laterza.

This criticism appeared in a noteworthy volume by [Emilio] Sereni, *Il capitalismo nelle campagne, 1860-1900* (Turin, 1947), which was written as part of a broader work in the years just before the outbreak of World War II.

Sereni's book did not find too favorable a reception among historians, perhaps because of the somewhat hasty manner in which it set forth information, its lack of original research, its excessively Marxist phraseology, and the error of some of its arguments (such as that on the financial policy of the *Destra*,[1] regarding which one should note the criticisms by [Federico] Chabod). Moreover, its rather undeniably schematic nature led to a somewhat oversimplified and rough antithesis between a typically feudal, aristocratic type of property and a bourgeois, capitalistic type of property—as if such noblemen as the Cavours, Jacinis, and Ricasolis did not represent in one way or another the most advanced aspects of capitalism in Italy. But in spite of all of this, Sereni's book remains the work of a scholar who is the secure master of Marxism's basic contentions regarding the way in which capitalism develops, and who in the light of such historical theory has carried out a serious effort to reinterpret the development of Italian society during the first forty years after unification. For this reason it is regrettable that few people have followed in Sereni's footsteps. It is precisely from the Marxian theory regarding capitalistic development that Sereni drew the conception of the agrarian revolution as a phenomenon that is historically linked to the complete victory of a bourgeois revolution. It is in the failure of such a revolution to occur during the *Risorgimento* that Sereni discerns the origin of the limitations and of grave contradictions that have existed in the social and political life of the unified state.

Gramsci, for his part, has further developed this same thesis, seeking to crown the economic and social doctrinairism of ordinary Marxist stamp with a perfected vision of the historical and political relationships that existed between the two principal forces of the *Risorgimento*. In Gramsci's writing appear also echoes of the debates that previous "revisionist-minded" historians sought to arouse among Italian scholarly circles. He ascribes the supremacy of the moderates to the fact that the Action Party was unable to carry out its own policy in a coherently Jacobinic manner by incorporating into its program the social problems and goals of the peasants. And he frames this conception in a vision of Italian history that is dominated by the inability of the medieval Italian cities to resolve the conflict with the countryside that began to take shape after the first phase of the antifeudal alliance. The centuries of oppression in the countryside, the decline of creative ability, the failure of every political effort at unification (along with the closely connected cosmopolitanism of Italian culture and civilization) all hark back to this split, which thus remains at the root of the whole history of the country. For this reason, there is thoroughgoing political insistence on the need for an alliance of workers and peasants to produce a historical termination to an almost thousand-year-old problem in the history of the country and to provide a way to resolve its conflicts and basic problems.

[1] The political right in Italy—the grouping to which Cavour belonged and which dominated Italian public life until 1876.—*Ed.*

It certainly cannot be said that this thesis has been discussed exhaustively. To be sure, almost all the Marxist historians of the *Risorgimento* have adopted it as their point of departure for a series of detailed investigations. Yet, so far as I know, no one has raised in adequate fashion the serious historical and methodological problems it contains. And this is the case despite the serious objections to it that were immediately raised. Some of our most authoritative historians— from [Benedetto] Croce and [Carlo] Antoni to [Federico] Chabod—have pointed out an error in Gramsci's position that is common to all the various revisionist interpretations of the *Risorgimento* since the time of [Alfredo] Oriani, [Mario] Missiroli, and [Piero] Gobetti—interpretations which are characterized by recourse to abstract moral and political idealism and which arbitrarily assume that what actually occurred ought to have occurred in a different fashion.

Along with this is the basic anachronism that this type of judgment did not arise out of the actual history of the time but rather out of much later problems that have presented themselves to the historian. Chabod has vigorously pointed out this anachronism on the part of Gramsci. He has emphasized the connection between Gramsci's criticism of the *Risorgimento* and the practical problem that faced Italian socialists and communists after World War I when they tried to bring about an alliance between the urban working-class movement and the peasant masses who were largely controlled by the [Catholic-oriented] "white leagues."

On the other hand, it should be kept in mind that the Gramsci thesis was first formulated as a criticism of the Action Party on the level of historical and political coherency, and that it sought to emphasize the Action Party's inability to carry out its own battle in a revolution predicated on a Jacobinic alliance of the advanced bourgeoisie with the peasants —an alliance which alone would have permitted the Action Party to break away from the hegemony exercised by the moderates and achieve a "consequent" democratic revolution.

Basic to the entire thesis was the presupposition that there existed a peasant structure that could be mobilized for the purpose of a national and democratic revolution—that there existed an "objective" revolutionary possibility which the Italian Action Party, unlike the French Jacobins, was unable to bring into play but which nevertheless was very much in the picture. It is unnecessary to emphasize all the doubts and reservations that this notion of an "objective" structure existing apart from the awareness of the people of that era can arouse and does arouse among non-Marxist historians. But it is also true that if one wishes to take into account the unquestionable importance that the Gramsci thesis has assumed in the polemics pertaining to the *Risorgimento,* one must go beyond mere discussion of principles and seek to understand its author's thought in depth, within the framework of his own methodology— with the reservation that one may later try to translate the results of this analysis into an interpretation that possesses validity for intellectuals of different philosophical inspiration.

Thus apart from any general discussion of methodology, two basic questions should be raised with respect to the Gramsci thesis. The first relates to the real possibility of an agrarian revolution, to the actual existence, in other words, of an alternative course of action to that which the *Risorgimento* pursued. The second relates to the question whether such an alternative course would have produced an outcome somewhat more progressive than what actually resulted. The second question is no less important that the first, because Gramsci's criticism of the *Risorgimento* ruling class focuses precisely on the argument that the ruling class did not push to the limit all the possibilities for progress that were objectively present in the Italian situation; and especially because an accurate statement of the real problem of modern capitalistic development in Italy in the nineteenth century depends on a proper evaluation of the significance of the agrarian "revolution that was lacking" [*rivoluzione mancata*].

Despite the ever longer list of peasant insurrections and disturbances that modern historians—not only Marxist writers —are preparing for us; despite the indubitable existence of widescale misery and privation in a large portion of the Italian countryside, and the widespread persistence of feudal remnants, especially in the south; despite the existence of a peasant population of more than fifteen million people in 1860, of whom the larger part were either poor peasants, hired day-laborers [*braccianti*], or salaried workers [*salariati*], and the proposals that hitherto had been suggested for mobilizing this mass of people against the old absolutistic regimes; despite all this, it seems undeniable that the presumed alternative course remained outside the sphere of practical historical and political action.

This was true not so much because of any tenaciously reactionary spirit [*sanfedismo*] in the countryside (for such a spirit might conceivably have been overcome by laying down guidelines for solution of the problem of land tenure) as because of the basic historical conditions in which the *Risorgimento* was destined to unfold. Rather, it seems certain that any agrarian and Jacobinic revolution in Italy would have provoked an anti-Italian coalition on the part of all the great powers of Europe, for the powers were interested in maintaining a conservative social order and held to a concept of civilization and of international relations that was deeply hostile to agrarian revolutionary activity. The problem of international relations in this respect has been vigorously emphasized by Chabod.

Even Gramsci asked the question (and he answered it negatively) whether it was possible in Italy to have a Jacobinic-type revolution in view of the fact that Italy had not yet achieved "international freedom of action," that France was still the traditionally dominant power in Europe, and that the climate of European opinion had changed so markedly since 1815. But in this respect his thinking seems particularly contorted, almost as though he were reluctant to accept all the consequences stemming from the difficulties that he posed:

Even though the Le Chapelier Law and the Law of the Maximum had limited the Jacobin program of seeking by force to reawaken the energies of the French popular masses so as to ally them with the bourgeoisie, the program still appeared in 1848 as a threatening "specter," and this fact was cleverly exploited by Austria and the old governments, even by Cavour—to say nothing of the pope. Perhaps because of subjective (though not objective) factors, the bourgeoisie could no longer extend its hegemony over as wide a range of common people [in Italy] as it had in France; nevertheless, activity among the peasantry was certainly always possible.[2]

Let us leave aside the "subjective" or "objective" character of the reasons which prevented an alliance of the bourgeoisie with the great popular masses throughout Europe in the nineteenth century, in the sense that Gramsci meant. (For in considering the "subjective" or "objective" character of the reasons we would have to raise once again the entire problem of the relationship between bourgeois liberalism and the proletarian movement during that period.) It remains a fact that in Italy's case, the hostility of all the great powers toward any agrarian uprising presented itself in a most "objective" fashion. It is therefore curious that one should affirm the possibility of "action among the peasants" after having denied the possibility of extending the bourgeoisie's domination over the wide strata of the populace—especially when it is clear that the two things are in reality only one, as it is impossible to shift the question to the urban strata of the populace, over whom the Action Party had largely succeeded in acquiring leadership.

Moreover, one should consider the extreme difficulty of transforming southern Italy (which, because of its relationship between town and country, stood at the center of the Gramsci thesis) into a country of rural democracy or small-scale property ownership after all we now know of the results of the census takings and tax assessments of the past century. (One should note that because of the flexibility of rules, those censuses eliminated in the zones in question the obstacle of land income chargeable to the cultivator.) Moreover, the experiences of the various governmental agencies for land reform have demonstrated to even the most obtuse what large sums of capital and vast technical resources (which are of decisive importance in adapting, systematizing, and increasing land productivity, and which were nonexistent during the past century) are required to solve the problem even on a very limited scale. It is clear that we are discussing here precisely the creation of a rural democracy. For if one interprets the Gramsci thesis in the sense that it was an argument that the Action Party should have supported the peasants more openly in partitioning demesne lands or in revising ancient cut-throat contracts, one would not only distort Gramsci's explicit thought (which was based on a comparison of the Italian situation with the agrarian policy of the French Jacobins), but one would empty it of all interest for our discussion, because it is evident that such a policy would have led either to a general uprising to seize the land, or to defeat, especially in the more backward zones where the old feudal structures would have survived. At most, it would have left but a few traces devoid of historical interest. . . .

Certainly the Gramsci thesis has a scope that extends well beyond the data of economics and class structure. It involves an interpretation of the entire history of Italy. For the Sardinian writer [Gramsci] the agrarian revolution was a great mechanism for resolving the deep-seated conflicts in the country's history, a powerful unifying instrument for all of Italian society, which would create a

[2] Antonio Gramsci, *Il Risorgimento* (Turin: Giulio Einaudi Editore, 1949), pp. 87–88.

closer relationship between the State and the "national and popular" forces of cultured groups and society in general. Such a revolution, however, could not take place in the nineteenth century as a force hostile to the expansion of modern capitalistic relationships; it could take place only to the extent that it might be able to promote and even to identify itself with such capitalistic relationships (for certainly it could not make Italy into a country of peasants or of artisans in the way that was idealized by the *petit bourgeois* democrats of the early 1800s). Even in France, where the Revolution likewise laid the basis for a great democratic tradition and managed to bring the masses more intimately into the political life of the state than was the case in Italy, can one say that the agrarian revolution really achieved profound unity between city and countryside? The great revolutionary crises of the nineteenth century, in 1848 and in 1871, showed what a deep gulf separated the urban revolutionary masses from the tenaciously conservative small landowners who had come to the fore during the Great Revolution—and it was Marx himself who was among the first to underscore this fact. Doubtless in Italy too the gulf persisted and was no less deep. This is not surprising when we reflect that this gulf involved a problem that was a thousand years old, tenaciously rooted in the whole course of Italian history, and aggravated by the decadence and inertia that marked so many centuries of the history of our country—a problem that other more fortunate nations have resolved only by means of century-long processes. With good reason, therefore, we can doubt that even the revolution Gramsci espoused could have brought that solution.

Basically, the agrarian revolution assumed for Gramsci a value quite similar to the resolving and eschatological one that Marxism perceived in the proletarian revolution; and in its most intimate significance, in the position which it occupied in the feeling and spirit of Gramsci, it ended by identifying itself with this. This observation brings us back to the comments on historical methodology made by Croce, Antoni, and Chabod regarding the polemical and political nature of this theory, and hence its essentially antihistorical quality.

On another occasion we might take up Gramsci's specifically historical and political interpretation—namely, his assertion that the Action Party was substantially "directed" by the moderates, a statement which corresponds essentially to King Victor Emmanuel II's remark that he held the Action Party "in his pocket." In actual fact, the democratic alternative to the moderate solution was something that was quite real and politically feasible in 1860. Between August and September of that year the hypothesis of a march by Garibaldi on Rome in order to convene a constituent assembly there, with the further developments of a republican and democratic nature that this implied, seemed anything but impossible. And the results of Mack Smith's recent and very accurate work serve to confirm this thesis if they are rightly interpreted.

Suggestions for Further Reading

Orientation in the literature on the *Risorgimento* can be gained in such historiographical surveys as Catherine E. Boyd's section on Italy in *The American Historical Association Guide to Historical Literature*, ed. George F. Howe et al (New York, 1961), pp. 526-548; Agatha Ramm, *The Risorgimento*, in the booklet series of the Historical Association (London, 1963); Kent R. Greenfield, "The Historiography of the *Risorgimento* since 1920," *Journal of Modern History*, VII (March, 1935), 49-67; Charles F. Delzell, "Italian Historical Scholarship: A Decade of Recovery and Development, 1945–55," *Journal of Modern History*, XXVIII (December, 1956), 374-388; and Charles F. Delzell, *Italy in Modern Times: An Introduction to the Historical Literature in English,* forthcoming in the "Service Center for Teachers of History" series of the American Historical Association.

In French, the following guides are useful: Paul Guichonnet, *L'unité italienne*, no. 942 in the booklet series, "Que sais-je?" (Paris, 1961); and Walter Maturi, "Les états italiens," in *L'Europe du XIXe et du XXe siècle (1815–1870): Problèmes et interprétations historiques,* ed. Max Beloff et al (Milan, 1959), vol. II, pp. 643-704.

In Italian one should consult Walter Maturi, *Interpretazioni del Risorgimento: Lezioni di storia della storiografia,* with bibliographical updating by Rosario Romeo (Turin, 1962); *Nuove questioni di storia del Risorgimento e dell'unità d'Italia* (2 vols.; Milan, 1961); Ettore Rota (ed.), *Questioni di storia del Risorgimento e dell'unità d'Italia* (Milan, 1951); "Risorgimento italiano," in the *Dizionario enciclopedico italiano* (Rome, 1959), vol. X, pp. 434-435; the bibliographical notes in Giorgio Candeloro's Marxist-oriented, multivolumed *Storia dell'Italia moderna* (Milan, 1956 ff.); and Francesco Lemmi, *Il Risorgimento: Guida bibliografica* (Rome, 1926). The major specialized journal devoted to this field is the *Rassegna storica del Risorgimento italiano,* published quarterly in Rome since 1914 by the Istituto per la Storia del Risorgimento Italiano, which also holds annual congresses.

For the most part, English-language works on the *Risorgimento* that were published more than forty years ago are written from a predominantly politico-military and anti-clerical point of view. Some of these works continue to be worth reading. William R. Thayer, in addition to his enduring *Life and Times of Cavour* (2 vols.; Boston, 1914), wrote another two-volume work, *The Dawn of Italian Independence, 1814–1849* (Boston, 1893), which also reflects his Protestant bias and sympathy for liberal Italy. Emphasizing the romantic, military side of the *Risorgimento*, George Macaulay Trevelyan's widely read books remain classics of their type: *Garibaldi's Defence of the Roman Republic* (London, 1919); *Garibaldi and the Thousand* (London, 1919); *Garibaldi and the Making of Italy* (London, 1911); and *Manin and the Venetian Revolution of 1848* (London, 1923).

Noteworthy also are Bolton King's Mazzinian-inspired *A History of Italian Unity* (2 vols.; London, 1899); Pietro Orsi, *Modern Italy, 1748–1898* (New York, 1900) and *Cavour and the Making of Modern Italy, 1810–1861* (New York, 1914); Jessie White Mario, *The Birth of Modern Italy* (London, 1909), sympathetic to Garibaldi; Evelyn Martinengo-Cesaresco, *The Liberation of Italy, 1815–1870* (London, 1902), *Cavour* (London, 1898), and *Italian Characters in the Epoch of Unification* (London, 1890). More general in scope is Evelyn M. Jamison et al, *Italy, Medieval and Modern* (Oxford, 1919). There are English versions of many of Mazzini's essays, as well as of Garibaldi's *Autobiography* (3 vols.; London, 1889) and Francesco Crispi's *Memoirs* (3 vols.; London, 1912-1914). Of limited value now are R. M. Johnston, *The Roman Theocracy and the Republic, 1846–1849* (London, 1901) and R. DeCesare, *The Last Days of Papal Rome, 1850–1870* (Boston, 1909).

Among the important interpretations of the *Risorgimento* to appear in English during the years since World War I are Benedetto Croce's "idealistic" *History of Europe in the Nineteenth Century,* tr. by Henry Hurst (New York, 1933); Guido De-Ruggiero's comparative *History of European Liberalism,* tr. by R. G. Collingwood (London, 1927; Boston, 1959); Luigi Salvatorelli's *Concise History of Italy from Prehistoric Times to Our Own Day,* tr. by B. Miall (New York, 1939). All the above were written in the liberal tradition in tacit defiance of the Fascist ideology. J. A. R. Marriott, *Makers of Modern Italy,* originally published in London, 1889, was revised in a 1931 edition that ended with needlessly adulatory references to Mussolini, as did George B. McClellan's *Modern Italy: A Short History* (Princeton, 1933). In the liberal-democratic category can be placed Janet P. Trevelyan, *A Short History of the Italian People* (4th ed.; New York, 1951); Arthur J. Whyte, *The Evolution of Modern Italy* (Oxford, 1943), a narrative, politico-military history of the period, 1715–1930; Massimo

Salvadori's brief *Cavour and the Unification of Italy* (Princeton, 1961); René Albrecht-Carrié's impressionistic *Italy from Napoleon to Mussolini* (New York, 1950); H. Stuart Hughes' brilliant essay, *The United States and Italy* (Cambridge, Mass., 1953, 1964), which emphasizes the post-*Risorgimento;* E. W. Gladstone et al, *The Unification of Italy* (Oxford, 1955), designed for English preparatory schools; and H. Hearder and D. P. Waley's very compact but useful *A Short History of Italy: From Classical Times to the Present Day* (Cambridge, Eng., 1963). Written from a Catholic perspective, George F. and Joan Berkeley, *Italy in the Making, 1815–1849* (3 vols.; Cambridge, Eng., 1932-1940) is a substantial work.

Most stimulating (and controversial) of all the recent English studies of the *Risorgimento* have been those by Denis Mack Smith. His *Italy: A Modern History* (Ann Arbor, 1959), dealing with the period after 1861, professes to find fascistic symptoms in Italy long before World War I. His major monograph is *Cavour and Garibaldi, 1860: A Study in Political Conflict* (Cambridge, Eng., 1954). These works can be supplemented by his interpretive essay on the *Risorgimento* in volume X of the *New Cambridge Modern History* (Cambridge, Eng., 1960); his popularized *Garibaldi: A Great Life in Brief* (New York, 1956); and such articles as "Cavour and Parliament," *Cambridge Historical Journal,* XIII (1957), 37 ff.; "The Italian Peasants and the *Risorgimento,*" in *Italia e Inghilterra nel Risorgimento,* published in London, 1954, by the Istituto Italiano di Cultura; and "The Peasants' Revolt in Sicily," in *Studi in onore di Gino Luzzatto,* vol. III (Milan, 1950).

Other significant modern studies of leaders of the climactic phase of the *Risorgimento* are Arthur J. Whyte, *The Early Life and Letters of Cavour, 1810–1848* (London, 1925), based on Francesco Ruffini's biography of 1912; Whyte's *Political Life and Letters of Cavour, 1848–1861* (London, 1930), utilizing the published Cavour-Nigra correspondence and unedited documents in the Public Record Office; Gwilym O. Griffith's admiring *Mazzini: Prophet of Modern Europe* (London, 1932); Gaetano Salvemini's analytical *Mazzini*, tr. by I.M. Rawson (Stanford, 1956); Edward E. Y. Hales, *Mazzini and the Secret Societies: The Making of a Myth* (New York, 1956), which deals critically with his early life; Stringfellow Barr's rather slim *Mazzini: Portrait of an Exile* (New York, 1935); Michael S. J. Packe's able study of *Orsini: The Story of a Conspirator* (Boston, 1957); and William K. Hancock's solid study of *Ricasoli and the Risorgimento in Tuscany* (London, 1926). Raymond Grew, *A Sterner Plan for Italian Unity: A History of the Italian National Society* (Princeton, 1963), is an exhaustive investigation of the role played by that society in the annexation of central and southern Italy. George Carbone's essay, "The Long Detour: Italy's Search for Unity," in *Studies in Modern European History in Honor of Franklin C. Palm* (New York, 1956), explains how Carlo Cattaneo's federalistic, republican ideas were at last put into effect a century later.

The bitter controversy between Church and State can be explored in Edward E. Y. Hales' sympathetic studies of the papacy: *Revolution and Papacy, 1769–1846* (Garden City, 1960) and *Pio Nono: A Study in European Politics and Religion in the Nineteenth Century* (New York, 1954). S. William Halperin's scholarly *Separation of Church and State in Italian Thought from Cavour to Mussolini* (Chicago, 1937) and *Italy and the Vatican at War* (Chicago, 1939) can be supplemented for the later period by Richard A. Webster, *The Cross and the Fasces: Christian Democracy and Fascism in Italy* (Stanford, 1960), and by Arturo C. Jemolo, *Church and State in Italy, 1850–1950*, tr. by David Moore (Oxford, 1960), an abridgment of a major study by an Italian liberal Catholic.

A pioneering work in the economic aspects of the *Risorgimento* is Kent R. Greenfield, *Economics and Liberalism in the Risorgimento: A Study of Nationalism in Lombardy, 1814–1848* (Baltimore, 1934). Shepard B.

Clough, *Economic History of Modern Italy* (New York, 1964), is the best general survey in English. An able discussion and critique of Rosario Romeo's rebuttal to the communist Gramsci thesis regarding the *Risorgimento* as an agrarian *rivoluzione mancata* is contained in Alexander Gerschenkron, *Economic Backwardness in Historical Perspective: A Book of Essays* (Cambridge, Mass., 1962), pp. 72–118. On the historiographical repercussions of the Gramsci thesis, see also A. William Salomone, "The *Risorgimento* between Ideology and History: The Political Myth of '*Rivoluzione Mancata*,' " *American Historical Review*, LXVIII (October, 1962), 38–56, and his "Statecraft and Ideology in the *Risorgimento*," *Italica*, XXXVIII (1961), 163-194.

Labor and socialistic currents can be studied in Richard Hostetter, *The Italian Socialist Movement, Vol. I: Origins, 1860–1882* (Princeton, 1958); Maurice F. Neufeld, *Italy: School for Awakening Countries: The Italian Labor Movement in Its Political, Social and Economic Setting from 1800 to 1960* (Ithaca, 1961); and Daniel L. Horowitz, *The Italian Labor Movement* (Cambridge, Mass., 1963).

Aspects of international relations are discussed in A. J. P. Taylor, *The Italian Problem in European Diplomacy, 1847–1849* (Manchester, 1934) and *Struggle for Mastery in Europe, 1848–1918* (Oxford, 1954); Howard M. Smyth, "The Armistice of Novara: A Legend of a Liberal King," *Journal of Modern History*, VII (June, 1935), 141–182; Derek E. D. Beales, *England and Italy, 1859–1860* (London, 1961); Miriam B. Urban, *British Opinion and Policy on the Unification of Italy, 1856–1861* (Scottdale, Pa., 1938); Noel Blakiston (ed.), *The Roman Question: Extracts from the Dispatches of Odo Russell from Rome, 1858–1870* (London, 1962); Lynn M. Case, *Franco-Italian Relations, 1860–1865: The Roman Question and the Convention of September* (Philadelphia, 1932) and *French Opinion on War and Diplomacy during the Second Empire* (Philadelphia, 1954); S. William Halperin, *Diplomat under Stress:*

Visconti-Venosta and the Crisis of July 1870 (Chicago, 1963); Lillian P. Wallace, *The Papacy and European Diplomacy, 1869–1878* (Chapel Hill, N.C., 1948); Howard R. Marraro, *American Opinion on the Unification of Italy* (New York, 1932) and *Diplomatic Relations between the United States and the Kingdom of Two Sicilies, 1816–1861* (2 vols.; New York, 1951–1952); and Mary P. Trauth, *Italo-American Diplomatic Relations, 1861–1882* (Washington, 1958).

Some of the early phases of the *Risorgimento* are examined in Gaudens Megaro's brilliant *Vittorio Alfieri, Forerunner of Italian Nationalism* (New York, 1930); Emiliana P. Noether's broadly conceived *Seeds of Italian Nationalism, 1700–1815* (New York, 1951); R. M. Johnston's outdated *The Napoleonic Empire in Southern Italy and the Rise of the Secret Societies* (2 vols.; London, 1904); and in the following monographs by R. John Rath, *The Fall of the Napoleonic Kingdom of Italy* (New York, 1941); George T. Romani, *The Neapolitan Revolution of 1820–21* (Evanston, Ill., 1950); and Joseph H. Brady, *Rome and the Neapolitan Revolution of 1820–21* (New York, 1937). Emphasizing gossipy court life, Harold Acton has sought to rehabilitate the *Bourbons of Naples (1734–1825)* (London, 1956) and the *Last Bourbons of Naples (1825–1861)* (London, 1961).

It is a pity that apart from a handful of titles by Croce, Salvatorelli, and one or two others, almost none of the important Italian studies of the *Risorgimento* that have appeared during the past forty years have been translated into English.[1] Students must read in their original version the works of such eminent Italian writers of the "liberal" school as Adolfo Omodeo, Walter Maturi, Franco Valsecchi, Alberto M. Ghisalberti, Nino Valeri, Federico Chabod, and many others. The federalistic, republican current of Carlo Cattaneo has been given belated sympathetic attention by the late Cesare Spellanzon and Ennio DiNolfo in their multivolumed and profusely illustrated work on the *Risorgimento*. Piero Pieri has finished a thorough military history of the *Risorgimento*, while Emilia Morelli, Alessandro Galante Garrone, and others have shed new light on Mazzinianism. Franco Venturi has studied the "circulation of ideas" in the Enlightenment, a theme followed up by Giorgio Vaccarino and Armando Saitta in their investigation of the impact of Jacobinism upon Italy. The neglected social and economic history of the era is attracting a larger number of scholars— for example, Rosario Romeo, Domenico Demarco, Luigi Bulferetti, Leo Valiani, Giacomo Perticone, and such communists as Guido Candeloro, Giuseppe Berti, Paolo Alatri, and others. Long-slighted religious aspects of the *Risorgimento* (Jansenism, Protestantism, and liberal Catholicism) are finding students like Arturo C. Jemolo, Giorgio Spini, Fausto Fonzi, and others. And, finally, a great deal of patient work is going on in the publication of collected works and correspondence of most of the major *Risorgimento* leaders.

[1] The same comment applies to most of the relevant studies in French (as well as other languages). Important works by Paul Matter, Paul Guichonnet, Maurice Vaussard, Jacques Godechot, A. Pingaud, Georges Bourgin, and others are unavailable in English.